THE THERAPIST'S NOTEBOOK on STRENGTHS and SOLUTION-BASED THERAPIES

THE THERAPIST'S NOTEBOOK ON STRENGTHS AND SOLUTION-BASED THERAPIES

Homework, Handouts, and Activities

BOB BERTOLINO
MICHAEL KIENER
RYAN PATTERSON

Routledge
Taylor & Francis Group
New York   London

Routledge
Taylor & Francis Group
270 Madison Avenue
New York, NY 10016

Routledge
Taylor & Francis Group
27 Church Road
Hove, East Sussex BN3 2FA

© 2009 by Taylor and Francis Group, LLC
Routledge is an imprint of Taylor & Francis Group, an Informa business

Printed in the United States of America on acid-free paper
10 9 8 7 6 5 4 3 2 1

International Standard Book Number: 978-0-415-99415-6 (Paperback)

Library of Congress Cataloging-in-Publication Data

Bertolino, Bob, 1965-
  The therapist's notebook on strengths and solution-based therapies : homework, handouts, and activities / Bob Bertolino, Michael Kiener, Ryan Patterson.
      p. cm.
  Includes bibliographical references and index.
  ISBN 978-0-415-99415-6 (pbk. : alk. paper)
  1. Solution-focused therapy--Problems, exercises, etc. I. Kiener, Michael. II. Patterson, Ryan. III. Title.

RC489.S65B473 2009
616.89'147--dc22
                                                                        2008050571

Visit the Taylor & Francis Web site at
http://www.taylorandfrancis.com

and the Routledge Web site at
http://www.routledgementalhealth.com

To Steve de Shazer and Insoo Kim Berg;
two seekers of solutions in life and beyond.

— Bob

To my parents, Cynthia and Jack, all of my efforts are possible
because of your unconditional love and support.

— Michael

To Youth in Need, you are an unceasing source of inspiration to me.

— Ryan

Contents

SECTION III   RECONNECTION TO SELF: EXPERIENCE, AFFECT, AND
EMOTION

SECTION IV   EXPLORING NEW WORLDS OF POSSIBILITY: CHANGING
PERSPECTIVES AND PERCEPTIONS

Acknowledgments

My deep appreciation to my family for living the ideas in this book. You always see possibilities and are unwavering in your love and support. A special thank you to my mom, Helen, and daughter, Morgan, for making me laugh, especially at myself. Thank you to Michael and Ryan for not just believing in these ideas but for seeing each moment as an opportunity to positively influence the lives of others. Thank you to Terry Trepper for the original vision of this work and George Zimmar, publisher at Routledge Mental Health, for your commitment and guidance with the project.

— Bob Bertolino

My heartfelt thanks to my friend Bob for his wisdom, support, and mentorship. And, as always, my undying appreciation to my family for their love and support.

— Ryan Patterson

Thank you to the staff and faculty at Maryville University, the staff at Youth in Need, Inc. and the St. Patrick Center, and to our friends, clients, and supporters who encourage us each and every day.

— Bob Bertolino
— Michael Kiener
— Ryan Patterson

Introduction

Effective therapists evoke, tap into, and employ client strengths and resources, recognizing that clients are the most important contributors to outcome (Orlinsky, Rønnestad, & Willutzki, 2004; Tallman & Bohart, 1999). This book offers multiple pathways for those in helping relationships to employ strengths and solution-based (SSB) principles and practices as a vehicle for promoting positive change with individuals, couples, and families. In this introductory chapter, we will

- Provide a brief discussion of the background of SSB
- Discuss the core principles of SSB
- Describe the format of this book
- Discuss how to use the exercises

Expanding the Field: A Brief Background of Strengths and Solution-Based (SSB) Ideologies

In the late 1970s and early 1980s, solution-based therapies (that is, solution-focused and solution-oriented therapies) represented a shift in perspective among therapists (de Shazer, 1985, 1988, 1991; O'Hanlon & Weiner-Davis, 2003) from focusing on problems and problem-talk to solutions and solution-talk. Central to this notion was the idea that there were exceptions to problems (times when they were diminished in their intensity or were absent altogether). A second tenet was that there were things that were already working in people's lives that should be encouraged, while things that were not should be the focus of attention. The way to foster change, however, was not by correcting deficits but by building on clients' strengths.

The idea of focusing on strengths was not unique to solution-based therapies. Strengths-based approaches had gained momentum in various disciplines outside of traditional psychology and psychotherapy circles to include family therapy and social work (Bertolino & O'Hanlon, 2002; Madsen, 2007; Rapp, 1998; Saleeby, 2006). An important distinction to be made was that the original solution-based approaches were developed as models, whereas strengths-based ideas represented more of a philosophical viewpoint that fueled these models (see Bertolino, 2010). Although this remains somewhat of a point of debate, it is clear that most effective approaches, not just solution-based therapies, are now underscored by principles that emphasize client strengths and encourage processes that build capacity. It can be said, then, that strengths-based ideas are synonymous with numerous models. This is encouraging given that research has demonstrated that clients' abilities and strengths are primary factors in therapeutic outcome.

Principles of Strengths and Solution-Based Therapies

The exercises in this book are based on a series of core principles that are not only central to solution-based therapies, but they have also been demonstrated through research to be essential to successful outcome (Bertolino, 2010). An SSB approach is founded on a series of core characteristics that reflect a philosophical posture of therapists. This includes a focus on processes and practices that are supported by research and are collaborative, competency based, culturally sensitive, client driven, outcome informed, and change oriented. The following are core principles of SSB.

Client Contributions

Clients are the most important contributors to outcome, accounting for as much as one-third to one-half of the overall variance in outcome (Lambert, 1992; Wampold, 2001). Client contributions include their internal strengths and external resources.

The Therapeutic Relationship and Alliance

Clients who are engaged and connected with their therapists are likely to benefit most from therapy (Orlinsky, Grawe, & Parks, 1994; Orlinsky, Rønnestad, & Willutzki, 2004). SSB is based on collaborative client–therapist partnerships in which clients' views about therapy processes, goals, and tasks to accomplish those goals are accommodated.

Cultural Competence

Cultural competence translates to having the capacity to function effectively in other cultural contexts. It is reflected through awareness and practices that involve learning new patterns of behavior and effectively applying them in the appropriate settings. This requires valuing diversity, which means accepting and respecting differences. People come from different backgrounds, and their customs, thoughts, ways of communicating, values, traditions, and institutions vary accordingly. Attention is given to the importance of the various influences that affect all aspects of therapy, including but not limited to creating safe, nurturing, and respectful contexts that encourage and facilitate growth and change.

Change as a Process

The principle of focusing on change as a process is characterized by three points: (1) focus is on enhancing change as opposed to searching for explanations about the nature of problems; (2) change is constant—people, situations, and problems are not static; and (3) change is predictable. These points are key considerations in working to promote growth in the form of possibilities and solutions.

Expectancy and Placebo

Both clients' and therapists' expectations about therapy affect change. This refers to the portion of improvement derived from clients' knowledge of being treated, the installation of hope, and the credibility the client places on the rationale and techniques used (Duncan, Miller, & Sparks, 2004). Effective therapists not only maintain an awareness of expectancy and hope, they also focus on ways of increasing these factors in all aspects of services. This includes a belief in what they do and how they practice.

Method and Factor of Fit

All approaches make use of methods and techniques. What is important is the degree or "factor of fit" between therapists' approaches and clients' ideas. Therapists take care to select methods that are respectful, are culturally sensitive, and fit with clients' beliefs about problems and about how change might occur. In addition, methods used in therapy should tap into the other five principles listed.

   The principles of SSB outlined do not exist independent of one another. They are interrelated—each part of a matrix that creates a foundation that is characterized by collaboration, competency, and change.

   The principles also represent an overarching philosophy, not a theory. SSB is based on a lens of capacity in which people are seen as having capabilities and resources within themselves and their social systems. When cultivated, activated, and integrated with new experiences, understandings, ideas, and skills, these strengths help people to reduce pain and suffering, resolve concerns and conflicts, and cope more effectively with life stressors. This contributes to an improved sense of well-being and quality of life, and higher levels of relational and social functioning. SSB practitioners promote change through respectful educational, therapeutic, and operational processes and practices that encourage and empower others (Bertolino, 2009).

The Format of This Book

The 90 plus exercises in this book are categorized into 7 sections as follows.

Section I—Becoming Strengths and Solution-Based: Creating a Context for Change

This section begins with exercises and activities aimed at increasing personal understanding of core values, including their influence on therapy. This involves reexamination of one's worldview, including personal assumptions about people and change. What follows are exercises that focus on ways of creating contexts for collaborative practice prior to the start of face-to-face therapy and in its opening moments. The more clients are engaged in therapy, the more likely they are to benefit. Also in this section are exercises that draw attention to the influence of language and terminology. This includes ways of conveying respect, acknowledging, and opening possibilities for solutions through conversation.

Section II—Getting Focused: Exploring Strengths and Solutions in Information Gathering

This second part begins a process of incorporating key aspects of SSB therapies. This section delves into numerous areas that give shape and direction to therapy. It begins with ways of opening space for clients' stories and comes to a close with exercises for selecting and matching strategies and methods offered in future parts. In between these bookends are exercises that focus on goal setting, outcomes, action and solution-talk, defining and understanding clients' concerns and problems, and evoking and eliciting strengths and resources to address challenges. The exercises in this part are pivotal for their role in engaging clients in conversations to identify and utilize their strengths and social support systems, enhancing change-affecting processes, and tracking the effectiveness of therapy.

Section III—Reconnection to Self: Experience, Affect, and Emotion

A frequently underemphasized aspect of change in solution-based therapies is the role of internal experience, which is characterized by affect, feelings, emotions, sensory experiences, and sense of self. For some clients, however, the primary pathway to change will be by connecting, reconnecting, increasing awareness of, or more fully experiencing their internal experiences. Although it is not always necessary for people to focus on their emotions, it can lead to greater degrees of relaxation, self-understanding, and fulfillment in life. In this part, readers will be offered activities aimed at enhancing internal experience (i.e., feelings and emotions) as a path to healing and change. Also in this chapter are ways of reestablishing connections to self and changing sensory experience (i.e., visual, auditory, and kinesthetic experience).

Section IV—Exploring New Worlds of Possibility: Changing Perspectives and Perceptions

A fundamental focus of SSB therapies is on the perspectives and perceptions that people hold. Sometimes these views are supportive and help people to move forward, and other times they contribute to being "stuck." This part of the book offers exercises aimed at helping clients to shift their patterns of attention, assumptions, evaluations, points of view, and identity stories through solution-talk. This can lead to a rewriting of their life stories and contribute to a new sense of self. Acknowledging and amplifying clients' new sense of self is a natural progression from addressing affect, experience, and emotion, and can open further possibilities.

Section V—Lives in Motion: Changing Patterns of Action and Interaction

Behavioral and interactional (family systems) approaches emphasize the importance of helping people to change what they do on an individual basis and in relation to one another. Solution-based approaches also focus on *how* and *what* people can do differently. This means employing searching for exceptions and solutions instead of continuing in the same problematic patterns. This part offers exercises and activities for identifying and altering problem patterns and implementing new, more effective ways of acting and interacting. Clients' strengths and resources are tapped into to bring about small changes that, in turn, can lead to bigger ones. Activities in this chapter emphasize smaller changes and the "doing" problems with an eye on creating "ripples" or larger systemic changes. Many of the ideas are particularly useful with couples and families.

Section VI—Narratives of Transformation: Change, Progress, Transitions, and Endings

Effective therapists show interest in and make efforts to monitor the progress their clients are making. Working with clients to recognize changes they have made and evaluating what needs to happen, from their perspective, to continue change is central to clients' ability to successfully manage their lives. It is important for clients and therapists to assess change and to evaluate and plan what needs to happen "next." Readers of this chapter are introduced to ways of approaching subsequent interactions and sessions, identifying and amplifying change, and managing setbacks and stuck points. This pivotal section assists practitioners with processes designed to build on change and further encourage hope so that clients become agents of their change.

Section VII—Creating a Culture of Care and Respect: Consultation, Supervision, and Development

SSB principles and practices are also advantageous and beneficial to work situations in all organizations. Working in strength-based ways will promote a culture of growth and acceptance that will support consultation and development. This includes exercises for use in consultation, supervision, staff development, and organizational growth. This final section also focuses on ways of expanding on the exercises in this book.

How to Use the Exercises in This Book

The exercises in this book are all formatted similarly to ensure easy accessibility. Each exercise includes the following:

1. Therapist's Overview
   a. Purpose of the Exercise
   b. Suggestions for Use
2. Exercise

The "Therapist's Overview" part is intended to provide the rationale behind the exercise and a synopsis of the exercise. The "Purpose of the Exercise" and "Suggestions for Use," including possible cross-references are also included in this part. These are other exercises that may be paired together along with any prerequisites to the exercise at hand.

The exercises can, but do not always, follow a sequence. Most exercises can be used at different junctures in therapy and can be modified as needed. In addition, many exercises can be used outside of therapy settings or as tasks. It is important to keep in mind that the use of the term "homework" may not fit well with some clients and can arouse negative experiences. It may therefore be more helpful to frame exercises as "experiments." By using the term "experiment," room is left to modify or change some aspect of the exercise or to do something completely different (Bertolino & Schultheis, 2002). This can also place more emphasis on clients' contributions to change processes and shift attention away from therapists as experts.

The selection of exercises should be a collaborative endeavor. Exercises are always to engender choice and flexibility, with therapists offering a smorgasbord of possibilities that emphasize clients' voices. Clients have a say-so in selection and may pass on the ideas presented or come up with something on their own. In the same vein, the more involvement clients have, the greater the likelihood of follow-through, excitement, and potential benefit.

It can be helpful to introduce the idea of trying an exercise as a way of "changing things up" and "being creative." Another consideration is to set up exercises through stories or examples of others who have benefited. We do not approach exercises as answers, only as ways of opening up new pathways with possibilities. We take care not to imply that an exercise will work, as an unsuccessful outcome can lead to clients feeling like failures or that their problems are really worse than previously thought. We want to create, not diminish, hope.

Follow-up to exercises is critical. When clients have tried an activity or exercise, it is important to talk with them about how it went and what happened. Consider questions that help to determine if the concern or problem got better or worse (be specific), what part or parts worked to any degree, what was learned, and what needs to happen next. This form of feedback informs future directions and whether goals are being met, if modification is necessary, whether an entirely new approach or activity is called for, or whether a move away from exercises altogether is necessary.

The exercises in this book are tools meant to enhance therapy. All exercises should tap into the core principles outlined at the beginning of this Introduction and offer a good "fit" for clients. The ultimate decision to do or not do an exercise is left up to the client. As therapists, we also bear in mind that if something does not work, we do not do more of the same. We do something different with an eye on helping clients to improve their well-being, relationships, and social roles.

We now invite you to explore the possibilities that await you and your clients. Our hope is that the exercises in this book will stimulate new pathways to solutions.

We Are Only as Strong as Our Weakest Link: Strengthening the Use of This Book

Therapist's Overview

Purpose of the Exercise

When embracing the principles of the systems approach (all things are interconnected to smaller and larger systems, and change in one part of the system impacts the entire system) and recognizing its connection to strengths and solution-based counseling, the phrase "we are only as strong as our weakest link" has significant relevance. Asking yourself what makes up your therapeutic system and how to collaborate with all involved to capitalize on its total resources is a large step that can be made in strengthening the chain of change.

The purpose of this exercise is to examine how this book fits into your therapeutic system and explore ways to link exercises together to utilize this book to its fullest. This book is designed to help you develop your skills as a helping professional, build therapeutic relationships, and strengthen client resources in all areas of their lives.

Suggestions for Use

1. This exercise is most appropriate as a tool to plan and reflect on sessions.
2. This exercise can also be utilized in supervision or as a teaching model for new counselors.
3. This exercise will be best used in conjunction with exercise VII.10, "Reinventing the Cookbook: Proactive and Reflective Ways to Use This Book."

Exercise

If you have not done so already, review the entire book to get a "feel" for its content. Next, try to think about this book beyond only a tool to be used when you are "stuck" with a client. Envision your therapeutic system and how you can incorporate the book into your system to maximize its effectiveness. Below are additional questions to think about as you use this text.

1. Think about this book in relation to the other books you find most helpful. How does it complement and provide new information to your counseling?

_____

_____

2. How does the material in the book complement the agency where you are working?

_____

_____

3. How does this book add to the other resources you use in your everyday work?

_____

_____

4. What questions remain unanswered after reading this text?

_____

_____

5. In general how do you think this material will be received by the clients you are working with?

_____

_____

6. What will make this material more effective with the clients you work with?

_____

_____

7. What exercises do you think will work most effectively together?

_____

_____

8. If you were to create your own exercise, how would it "fit" into your therapeutic system?

_____

_____

Try to modify existing exercises to meet the individual needs of your clients.

References

Bertolino, B. (2010). *Strengths-based engagement and practice.* Boston: Allyn & Bacon.

Bertolino, B., & O'Hanlon, B. (2002). *Collaborative, competency-based counseling and therapy.* Boston: Allyn & Bacon.

Bertolino, B., & Schultheis, G. (2002). *The therapist's handbook for families: Solution-oriented exercises for working with children, youth, and families.* New York: The Haworth Press.

de Shazer, S. (1985). *Keys to solution in brief therapy.* New York: Norton.

de Shazer, S. (1988). *Clues: Investigating solutions in brief therapy.* New York: Norton.

de Shazer, S. (1991). *Putting difference to work.* New York: Norton.

Duncan, B. L., Miller, S. D., & Sparks, J. A. (2004). *The heroic client: A revolutionary way to improve effectiveness through client directed, outcome-informed therapy* (Revised paperback edition). San Francisco: Jossey-Bass.

Lambert, M. J. (1992). Implications of outcome research for psychotherapy integration. In J. C. Norcross & M. R. Goldfried (Eds.), *Handbook of psychotherapy integration* (pp. 94–129). New York: Basic Books.

Madsen, W. C. (2007). *Collaborative therapy with multi-stressed families* (2nd ed.). New York: Guilford.

O'Hanlon, W. H., & Weiner-Davis, M. (2003). *In search of solutions: A new direction in psychotherapy* (2nd ed.). New York: Norton.

Orlinsky, D. E., Grawe, K., & Parks, B. K. (1994). Process and outcome in psychotherapy—NOCH EINMAL. In A. E. Bergin & S. L. Garfield (Eds.), *Handbook of psychotherapy and behavior change* (4th ed., pp. 270–378). New York: Wiley.

Orlinsky, D. E., Rønnestad, M. H., & Willutzki, U. (2004). Fifty years of process-outcome research: Continuity and change. In M. J. Lambert (Ed.), *Bergin and Garfield's handbook of psychotherapy and behavior change* (5th ed., pp. 307–390). New York: Wiley.

Rapp, C. A. (1998). *The strengths model: Case management with people suffering from severe and persistent mental illness.* New York: Oxford University Press.

Saleeby, D. (2006). *The strengths perspective in social work practice* (4th ed.). Boston: Allyn & Bacon.

Tallman, K., & Bohart, A. (1999). The client as a common factor: Clients as self-healers. In M. A. Hubble, B. L. Duncan, & S. D. Miller (Eds.), *The heart and soul of change: What works in therapy* (pp. 91–132). Washington, DC: American Psychological Association.

Wampold, B. E. (2001). *The great psychotherapy debate: Models, methods, and findings*. Mahwah, NJ: Lawrence Erlbaum Associates.

SECTION I

BECOMING STRENGTHS AND SOLUTION-BASED
Creating a Context for Change

I.1 The Philosophical Inventory: Expanding Awareness and Impact of Beliefs

Therapist's Overview

Purpose of the Exercise

There are many influences that contribute to the lenses through which we view and experience the world. Although some are (or will be) more meaningful than others, each influence makes a contribution to the formation of our respective personal philosophies. These philosophies affect change, preceding therapy models and theories, giving shape to methods, and informing service provision. Because our personal philosophies are constantly evolving, it is crucial to remain open to the process of reexamining beliefs. Philosophy, the blueprint of our belief systems, however, is frequently the point from which impossibility originates. It arguably poses the most significant threat to helping relationships. It can lead to increased stress, decreased job motivation, dissatisfaction, decreased effectiveness, resentment, anxiety, depression, physical illness, burnout, and, ultimately, the loss of hope. Some philosophies open up possibilities for change, whereas others close them down and can threaten both those providing and those receiving services. The purpose of this exercise, therefore, is to help you gain a more intimate understanding of your beliefs.

Suggestions for Use

1. This exercise is primarily for therapists. It can be modified for use with clients.
2. This exercise can be used periodically to explore beliefs and how they may be influencing therapy processes.

Exercise

This exercise is to help in identifying underlying beliefs and their influence on therapy processes. To complete this exercise, please answer the questions listed below in Parts I and II. It may also be helpful to discuss your responses with colleagues or others as a means of deepening your understanding of the role of philosophy in therapy.

Part I

1. What core beliefs or assumptions do you have about people and change?

_____

_____

_____

2. How have you come to believe what you believe and know what you know?

_____

_____

_____

3. What have been the most significant influences on your beliefs?

_____

_____

_____

_____

4. To the best of your knowledge, how have your beliefs and assumptions affected your work with people? With colleagues? With the community?

_____

_____

_____

_____

5. Do you believe that positive change is possible even with the most "difficult" and "challenging" people? (If you answered "yes," proceed to Question 6. If you answered "no," proceed to Question 8.)

_____

_____

_____

_____

6. How, in your view, do you believe that change occurs?

_____

_____

_____

_____

7. What do you do to promote change? (If you answered this question, end here.)

_____

_____

_____

8. How do you work with others with the belief they cannot change?

_____

_____

_____

_____

9. If you do not believe that the people with whom you work can change, what keeps you in the field?

_____

_____

_____

_____

Part II

1. What did you learn about yourself?

_____

_____

_____

_____

2. What did you learn about your philosophy of change?

_____

_____

_____

_____

3. How do you think your views impact your work in helping relationships?

_____

_____

_____

4. What, if any, new thoughts do you have about how your philosophy could become more of a vehicle for change for you and the people with whom you work or will work with in the future?

_____

_____

_____

_____

5. What might you do with this information?

_____

_____

_____

_____

I.2   Dismantling Your Status Quo: Challenging Assumptions and Gaining Insight

Therapist's Overview

Purpose of the Exercise

When discussing why clients do not attend a session, it is sometimes heard, "it is the population." Although a clinician may never know the true reason why a client "no shows," it is important to ask questions and not just assume "it is the population." Moreover, dismantling individual status quos will help the investigation of all aspects of practice to help ensure an effective therapeutic relationship.

The purpose of this exercise is to increase abilities to become a reflective practitioner while identifying strengths and areas of improvement. The more that is understood about the counseling worldview, the more that strengths can be utilized to collaborate with clients to create and sustain change.

Suggestions for Use

1. This exercise may be useful for self-reflection and didactic or group supervision.
2. This exercise may help in assessing how participation and facilitation are impacting the client's process of change.
3. This exercise may be used as a tool for planning future sessions.
4. This exercise is also very beneficial as a supervision task.

Exercise

To complete this exercise, think about your counseling and answer the questions below.

1. When you think of an ideal client, what comes to mind?

_____

_____

2. What personal characteristics or values do you have that make you think this person is an ideal client?

_____

_____

3. How will your characteristics and values make you an effective counselor with this client?

_____

_____

4. When you think of a challenging client, what comes to mind?

_____

_____

5. What personal characteristics or values do you have that make you think this person is a challenging client?

_____

_____

6. How could your characteristics and values regarding your challenging clients hinder your effectiveness?

_____

_____

7. Reflect back to a client you felt terminated early; what was the circumstance of the termination?

_____

_____

8. What role did you play in the early termination?

_____

_____

9. How can you take what you learned about yourself and improve your counseling?

_____

_____

Not only is it important to reflect on aspects of counseling that can be improved, it is equally important to reflect on aspects of counseling that are not typically questioned. This reflection can reveal blind spots in clinical practice.

I.3   *Creating New Meaning: All Our Actions Are Meaningful*

Therapist's Overview

Purpose of the Exercise

Counseling is often described as a conversation. Defining counseling in this fashion seems to normalize the process for those who believe they are ill prepared to begin counseling. Conversations are everyday occurrences and powerful tools to convey meaning. Individuals communicate and transmit meaning in many different ways, both verbal and nonverbal. Thus, counseling can serve as an excellent means to create new meaning for all involved. The purpose of this exercise is to examine how counselors and clients use language to communicate and create meaning in their lives.

If language is the primary tool counselors use, it would seem beneficial to examine what goes into a "good" conversation and ways to utilize its effectiveness. If talking is half of a conversation, then listening is the other. Equal importance also needs to be placed on counselor listening skills. It is essential to know when and what to say and to also know when not to say anything. Simple activities can be used to improve both verbal and nonverbal skills. From an SSB perspective, reframing a client's experience to highlight strengths and resources is an excellent means to begin the change process. Stating client concerns in past tense is a subtle way to indicate the concern is in the past, and it opens up the possibility for a new reality. To improve nonverbal and listening skills, try engaging a friend in conversation and see how long the conversation will last without talking. To keep the conversation moving, use head nods, eye contact, and simple phrases like "uh ums" and "tell me more."

Suggestions for Use

1. This exercise may benefit beginning counselors as a means to develop how they use language in sessions. It can also be used as a tool in supervision to reflect and improve on language use.
2. The intent of this exercise can be used early on in counseling to establish a strong therapeutic relationship.
3. Older adolescents and adults may benefit most from this exercise.

Exercise

Here are some questions to be answered by the counselor that will enable a more successful use of verbal and nonverbal language.

1. How would you classify your counseling style—are you more of a talker or a listener?

_____

_____

2. How can you develop your style to maximize your strengths and still create change with your client?

_____

_____

Practice stating client concerns in past tense and reframing them as goals, for example: "You stated you felt depressed last week. What would be one sign in the upcoming week to tell you things are a little bit better?"

Start to notice how your clients communicate—are they verbal or nonverbal, do they keep eye contact, do they have long periods of silence between thoughts? Noticing how your clients communicate and matching their preferred communication style will go a long way toward a successful session.

When communicating with your client, try to use action phrases to amplify change and use language that will presuppose change, for example: "How will you know when things get just a bit better?" "How are things better since the last time we met?" "Now that you are working toward change, how do you view your progress?" and "You stated in the past that you have never lasted this long without a setback; what do you account for sustaining this change?"

Here are a few further suggestions to think about...

Although language is perhaps the greatest tool a counselor has, it is equally important to focus on being genuine and empathetic. A client will soon be able to tell the difference between a counselor who uses strength-based language but is not empathetic and one who is both empathetic and uses strength-based language. Nonverbal messages transmit as much meaning as verbal messages.

Another tip that may be helpful is asking clients their communication preference. For example, if a client is overly silent, ask the client if he or she is thinking of a response or question or if he or she wants a question or response from me.

I.4 Taking the "ic" Out of the Person: Seeing the Core Within

Therapist's Overview

Purpose of the Exercise

Some have difficulty defining themselves beyond their given diagnosis or disability, for example: "Hi my name is Jim and I am a schizophrenic." From a rehabilitation counseling perspective, that is called salience of a disability or diagnosis. When an individual has a mental illness or disability, often through stigma and lack of full inclusion into society, his or her disability or diagnosis becomes the main identifier for that individual and others. The salience of a disability or diagnosis is also prevalent in agencies that embrace the medical model. Frequently, people are referred to as a diabetic, an epileptic, or a cancer patient. Rehabilitation agencies (and I would assume other agencies) adopted new terminology referred to as person-first language to describe people receiving services to shift emphasis from pathology to empowerment. Such names include consumer, member, participant, and individual. All the names have the intent to give control back to the individual and decrease the salience of the disability or diagnosis.

The purpose of this exercise is to recognize the impact language has on individual development. How individuals respond to others has a direct impact on how we view ourselves. When helping professionals place a heavy emphasis on deficits and pathology, individuals create identities of deficits and pathology. Helping professionals are in a unique position to dramatically change how people view disability and mental illness simply by recognizing language and the meaning it conveys. In addition to describing a person by his or her diagnosis, we often add value-laden or unnecessary words to describe the individual's experience. For example, even though Johnny has schizophrenia, he works a 40-hour week. Or, Mary Ellen suffered a stroke. In the first example, what does schizophrenia have to do with working 40 hours a week? It is our faulty assumptions that make us think people with mental illness cannot work or cannot work 40 hours. In the second sentence, how do we know Mary Ellen suffered? It is up to the person who had or experienced the stroke, heart attack, or illness to describe his or her experience.

Suggestions for Use

1. This exercise may be beneficial to use in supervision when examining how language is used to create meaning.
2. This exercise may also be beneficial as a component to discuss in an agency staffing. It could be how all individuals are viewed and perceived.
3. This exercise may be excellent to use in conjunction with other exercises that focus on language.

Exercise

After reading the purpose of the exercise, how would you change the following sentences?

1. Joe, who uses a wheelchair, is a wiz on the computer.

_____

_____

2. Because Joe is confined to his wheelchair, it is easy for him to sit at a computer desk.

_____

_____

3. Even though Julie has a disability, she is beautiful.

_____

_____

4. John suffered a traumatic brain injury when he was in a car accident at the age of 18.

_____

_____

5. John lost his leg during his service in the military.

_____

_____

6. The disabled veteran receives services from the VA hospital.

_____

_____

7. In addition to the visible defects, he suffers with a hearing impairment and wears thick eyeglasses.

_____

_____

I.5 *Composing Your Theoretical Worldview: What I Believe*

Therapist's Overview

Purpose of the Exercise

The purpose of this exercise is to gain a deeper understanding of individual values, beliefs, and biases, and how they impact counseling. By specifically writing values, an overt focus has been placed on personal beliefs. A secondary purpose is to gain awareness of individual ideas of change and how that integrates into SSB therapy.

Suggestions for Use

1. This exercise can be used with counselors in any stage of their career.
2. It can be used as a tool to develop and refine your skills.
3. This exercise can also be used to help prepare for job interviews—the more you will be able to articulate your beliefs, the more valuable you will be to an employer.

Exercise

To begin this exercise, think about your core beliefs about life and counseling. Think about how they have developed and how they will impact your professional career. For example, "I believe that all individuals have the capacity to change. I developed this belief because…, and this will help my counseling by…" You can also write your core belief statement as an action or an "if, then" statement. **If** I believe all individuals have the capacity to change, **then** I will do … while counseling. Completing this exercise will help you to identify your strengths and areas of improvement. Having a continual reflection on your counseling will allow you to not become complacent in your counseling and to focus on effectiveness.

Core Belief (1)

_____

    a. I believe this because:

_____

_____

    b. This belief will help my counseling by:

_____

_____

    c. Or: If I believe this _____, then I will do _____
       while counseling.

Core Belief (2)

_____

   a. I believe this because:

_____

_____

   b. This belief will help my counseling by:

_____

_____

   c. Or: If I believe this _____, then I will do _____
      while counseling.

Core Belief (3)

_____

   a. I believe this because:

_____

_____

   b. This belief will help my counseling by:

_____

_____

   c. Or: If I believe this _____, then I will do _____
      while counseling.

Core Belief (4)

_____

   a. I believe this because:

_____

_____

b. This belief will help my counseling by:

_____

_____

c. Or: If I believe this _____, then I will do _____
   while counseling.

Here are a few suggestions to think about after composing a theoretical worldview.

1. Every few months reflect on what you have written and make revisions as necessary.
2. Bring your theoretical worldview to supervision and use it as a discussion point.

I.6   Me, Myself, and I: Understanding Personal Strengths

Therapist's Overview

Purpose of the Exercise

Although known anecdotally for years, a growing body of research suggests that therapists' contributions to change are much more significant than previously thought. Often referred to as "therapist effects," what practitioners bring into the therapeutic milieu can be helpful in facilitating client change. Therapist contributions include personal strengths that can be tapped into to assist with thinking differently about situations, generating new ideas, remaining resilient when facing therapy challenges, and so on. The purpose of this exercise is to help therapists identify strengths that can be used as building blocks to help clients experience positive outcomes.

Suggestions for Use

1. This exercise is primarily for therapists. It can be modified for use with clients.
2. In identifying strengths, it can be helpful to think about other contexts in addition to therapy in which abilities were used to solve problems or find solutions. These abilities may have occurred just one time or repeatedly.

Exercise

Clients are not the only ones in the therapeutic milieu who have strengths. Therapists bring with them a host of abilities and resources that can go unnoticed and underutilized. This exercise will help you identify strengths in which you can tap and use actively with clients to facilitate positive change. To complete this exercise, answer the questions below by writing your responses in the spaces provided.

1. What do you do well as a therapist?

_____

_____

_____

_____

2. How have you developed those strengths or abilities?

_____

_____

_____

_____

3. How are those strengths useful to you as a therapist?

_____

_____

_____

4. What would others who have observed you or worked with you say that you do well?

_____

_____

_____

5. How might you increase your awareness of those abilities and use them a little more often as a therapist?

_____

_____

_____

_____

6. What is a skill that you use in other areas of your life but perhaps not so deliberately as a therapist? How might you transfer that skill to your work as a therapist?

_____

_____

_____

_____

7. What might you do in the future to further develop your strengths as a therapist?

_____

_____

_____

_____

Consider sharing your responses with colleagues or supervisors and perhaps including them as part of your professional development planning.

I.7   How I Describe What I Do: Examining Personal Theory and Principles of Change

Therapist's Overview

Purpose of the Exercise

Our expectations of clients, change, and therapy are shaped by numerous influences including culture, spirituality, family, and education. These contribute to our worldviews. For therapists, these influences also contribute to personal theories with principles about how and under what conditions we believe change will occur. Although not every therapist has examined his or her personal theory, it nonetheless influences how clients are approached. The purpose of this exercise is to help you, as a therapist, to articulate and examine your core theory of change and the principles that guide it. In addition, you will have an opportunity to explore how these beliefs correspond with the underlying principles that form the foundations of an SSB perspective.

Suggestions for Use

1. This exercise is for therapists or for any professional or student who works in the helping professions.
2. Because practitioners' personal theories evolve and change over time, it is important to periodically revisit this exercise.
3. Cross-reference: This exercise is best used in conjunction with Exercise I.1, "The Philosophical Inventory: Expanding Awareness and Impact of Beliefs."

Exercise

There are many influences that shape our theoretical approaches. Because our personal approaches or theories can either open up or close down possibilities for change, it is important to examine how they affect therapy. This exercise is to help you as a practitioner to articulate and examine your personal theory of therapy and the principles of change that inform it. You will also have an opportunity to explore how your theory compares to the foundational premises of an SSB-focused perspective. For this exercise, please complete Parts I and II by writing your answers in the spaces provided.

Part I

In one paragraph, write your personal theory of change. This should include how and under what conditions you expect your client to change.

_____

_____

_____

_____

_____

_____

_____

_____

_____

_____

_____

Next, write the basic assumptions or principles that guide your work with clients. Try to consolidate your theory to reflect a set of no more than eight general ideas.

1. _____

2. _____

3. _____

4. _____

5. _____

6. _____

7. _____

8. _____

Take some time to reflect on your personal theory and the underlying assumptions or principles you outlined. Consider the possible benefits and drawbacks or limitations. Next, write down the benefits under the "+" symbol and the limitations under the "–" symbol.

Part II

For the second part of this exercise, please refer to the six foundational premises of an SSB approach. These premises are listed below and are described in detail in the introduction. Recall that these principles are informed by research and reflect factors that were correlated with effective therapy outcomes. Consider how your theory and principles of change correspond with and align with those outlined. Then, in the spaces provided, list each principle you developed under the principle of SSB therapy that you believe best captures the essence of your principle. You may list more than one or not have any personal principles to list under the SSB principles below.

Strengths, Solution-Based Principles

1. Client Contributions

   My principle:_____

   _____

   My principle:_____

   _____

2. The Therapeutic Relationship and Alliance

   My principle:_____

   _____

   My principle:_____

   _____

3. Culture and Context

   My principle:_____

   _____

   My principle:_____

   _____

4. Change as a Process

   My principle:_____

   _____

   My principle:_____

   _____

5. Expectancy and Hope

My principle:_____

_____

My principle:_____

_____

6. Method and Factor of Fit

My principle:_____

_____

My principle:_____

_____

What did you learn from this exercise?

_____

_____

What might you do with this information?

_____

_____

I.8   The Key Is Collaboration: Working "With" Clients

Therapist's Overview

Purpose of the Exercise

The quality of the client's participation is an important factor in outcome. Therapists can increase client participation by working with, as opposed to on, clients in therapy. This involves inviting clients into conversations in which their preferences are learned and incorporated in therapy. The purpose of this exercise is to begin the process of collaborating with clients prior to the start of and in the opening moments of therapy. This is encouraged through the use of "collaboration keys."

Suggestions for Use

1. Consider the multiple ways that clients can be invited into collaborative conversations in which their preferences determine how therapy is carried out.
2. Although the ideas described offer possibilities for client engagement and strengthening relationships, there will be circumstances for which one or more ideas in this section will not be applicable in a particular context. In such instances, avoid offering a particular means of collaborating if it is not a possibility given the preestablished rules or parameters of a program or service. If it is possible to expand or negotiate the rules of a program or service, however, think creatively, consult with others, seek supervision, and always advocate for the best interests of clients.
3. Some forms of collaborative conversation can be utilized during phone conversations. Others will be better suited for face-to-face interactions.

Exercise

The quality of the client's participation is a critical factor in outcome. This suggests a focus on involving clients in all facets of services to better accommodate therapy to their needs. Here are eight collaboration keys and ways of doing this:

1. *Service Expectations*—Clients' expectations can affect how services progress and the degree to which they benefit. Therapists use strategies such as *creating space*, *preinterviews*, and *exploring/setting expectations* to learn and address clients' expectations.

2. *Attendance of Meetings/Sessions*—A factor that can inhibit positive change is when therapists' rules or preferences run counter to or do not match those of their clients. Therapists partner with clients to determine who should attend present and future sessions.

3. *The Format of Meetings/Sessions*—Therapists will have preconceived ideas and preferences about the format of sessions, including whether clients should be seen together (a unit or family), separately, and so on. Clients often have their own ideas and preferences that may differ from those of their therapists. Therapists partner with clients to determine which format provides the best fit.

4. *The Physical Space and Setting of Sessions*—The physical setting of sessions can be meaningful to clients and reflect beliefs associated with culture, ethnicity, and family background. Although the most common setting for therapy is in offices, there are other contexts, such as schools, homes, and prisons, where more and more services are being provided. Therapists strive to meet clients' setting expectations to create positive and beneficial therapy experiences.

5. *The Timing, Length, and Frequency of Sessions*—Client scheduling, related to the timing, length, and frequency of sessions, can raise issues for both therapists and clients. Therapists talk with clients about their preferences regarding which dates, days, and times of day are best to schedule meetings and sessions, and then they work to make reasonable accommodation when possible.

6. *The Open Door Perspective*—This refers to programming that offers reasonable access to people who are in immediate need, allowing for people to move in and out of therapy as necessary. This provides a fit for clients as they move through life stages and transitions and as their lives and needs change.

7. *Premeeting/Session Change*—People's problems fluctuate in frequency, intensity, and duration, providing opportunities to help identify subtle differences prior to first sessions. Either prior to or during initial sessions, therapists ask clients to notice any variations or improvements with the concerns that led them to seek therapy. Any differences are drawn out and explored as a means of facilitating positive change.

8. *Process and Outcome Informed*—Clients' perceptions of the therapeutic alliance are the most consistent predictor of outcome. Because higher client ratings of the therapeutic alliance yield better outcomes, therapists explore ways to incorporate client feedback in all aspects of therapy. *Process-oriented* feedback involves methods for eliciting and incorporating clients' perceptions of the therapeutic relationship and alliance. *Outcome-oriented* feedback relates to methods that monitor clients' perceptions of the impact of services. Therapists introduce and encourage both forms of client feedback and incorporate that feedback to strengthen the therapeutic alliance and increase the opportunities for a successful outcome.

By creating collaborative partnerships from the outset and maintaining them throughout services, we can tap into client contributions, attend to cultural influences, increase expectancy and hope, and enhance the change-affecting variables. The purpose of this exercise is to stimulate further questions that can be used in conjunction with the collaboration keys. To complete this exercise, please follow the directions below and write your responses in the spaces provided.

1. Create two questions for each of the collaboration keys listed.

   Addressing Service Expectations

   a. _____

   b. _____

   Determining Who Should Attend Meetings/Sessions

   a. _____

   b. _____

Determining the Format of Meetings/Sessions

a. _____

b. _____

Determining the Setting of Sessions

a. _____

b. _____

Determining the Timing, Length, and Frequency of Sessions

a. _____

b. _____

2. Create a brief narrative for introducing each of the following collaboration keys to clients.

Utilizing an Open Door Perspective

_____

_____

_____

Emphasizing Premeeting/Session Change

_____

_____

_____

Becoming Process Informed

_____

_____

_____

Becoming Outcome Informed

_____

_____

_____

I.9 *Expectations and Next-Pectations: Learning Clients' Preferences for Therapy*

Therapist's Overview

Purpose of the Exercise

Our expectations often lead the way as we enter into situations and relationships. In the same vein, clients will often enter therapy with current and future ideas ranging from how they expect therapy to occur to how they expect change to take place. By tuning into clients' ideas, we can learn more about how they believe therapy can be helpful and then work to match those expectations through therapy. The purpose of this exercise is to learn about clients' expectations as they begin therapy and then incorporate those perspectives from the start.

Suggestions for Use

1. This exercise can be used with individuals, couples, and families. Be reminded that with couples and families there are likely to be multiple and different perspectives represented. It may therefore be useful to have each person complete his or her own and then seek to identify common expectations and preferences.
2. Because clients' expectations can change over time, it is important to maintain ongoing conversations to monitor for those changes and incorporate new or modified expectations into therapy.
3. Cross-references: This exercise can be used in conjunction with Exercise I.8, "The Key is Collaboration: Working "With" Clients," and Exercise II.15, "In Many Ways: Mapping Paths of Change."

Exercise

Whether we are buying a car, getting a massage, or seeing a therapist, we enter services and relationships, specifically, with expectations. These may involve how we expect to be treated, what we expect to take place, what we would like to gain, and so on. This exercise can help you to clarify your expectations for therapy. This, in turn, can better prepare your therapist to be as helpful as possible in working with you to achieve the change you desire. To complete this exercise, please answer the questions below and write your answers in the spaces provided.

1. What are your expectations of therapy?

_____

_____

_____

2. What expectations, if any, do you have of a therapist?

_____

_____

_____

3. What ideas do you have about how therapy might help with your concern, problem, or situation?

_____

_____

_____

4. What kinds of things do you believe will help you in therapy to be successful with the concern(s) you are facing?

_____

_____

_____

5. What might you do if you find therapy unhelpful or if it is not proceeding a way you like?

_____

_____

_____

6. What else would you want a therapist to know about your expectations of therapy?

_____

_____

_____

I.10   The Body Knows: The Influence of Words

Therapist's Overview

Purpose of the Exercise

Words affect people in different ways. The effects of language on thinking and emotion are well documented. Language and interaction, however, can also affect physiology. We often do not fully recognize the impact words have on our physiological states. Some words can bring about negative physical experiences, such as heaviness in the body, tiredness, and even somatic sensations (for example, stomach upset, body tension). Others can lead to feeling physically stronger and experiencing increases in energy.

Researchers studied the effects of language, interaction, and significant events on both psychology and physiology. Some suggest that under certain conditions (for example, trauma, stress, threats, catastrophic events), the frontal cortex of the brain, which is responsible for thinking, speech, and language, becomes inhibited, thereby limiting a person's ability to reason and articulate thoughts. At the same time, portions of the area around the brain stem, including the amygdala and hypothalamus, which are responsible for physiological reactions, become increasingly active. This combination contributes to hyperarousal, affecting a person's ability to regulate emotion and think clearly. Others found that under perceived stress in relationships, people can experience physiological arousal and psychological shutdown. The result is that people may experience difficulty in self-soothing, regulating emotion, and responding in calm ways when under distress.

Finally, research suggests that language and different forms of vibration affect the molecular composition of water crystals. Water exposed to harsh, loud sounds or "negative energy" tended to fragment and present with disease-like qualities among the crystals. In contrast, the water exposed to soft, soothing sounds or "positive energy" revealed crystals that appeared to be growing and expanding. If water is affected by qualities such as vibration, tone, and volume, and the human body is estimated to be 70% water, the implications are vast. It seems that words have the capability to directly influence our physiological states beyond what might be expected through cognitive processes (in other words, something said to us that is perceived as negative in turn affects our physiology). This underscores the importance of subtleties communicated through voice tone, rate of speech, pitch, and body posture.

The purpose of this exercise is to better understand the effects of words, language, and interaction on people, particularly at the physiological level. By playing closer attention to not just the words but also how they are used, we can promote change and healing at multiple levels.

Suggestions for Use

1. This exercise can be used to work with clients on both the words they choose and how they say those words, as well as how others might perceive their words emotionally and physiologically (in their bodies). It can be useful in promoting the mind–body connection.

2. This exercise can be used in various ways by practitioners and clients, for example:

   a. The therapist can say various words out loud and have the client report what he or she experienced having heard them.
   b. Have the client repeat a list of words to another client (in a couple or family) and have the person receiving the words reflect on them.

   c. Have clients practice saying words to each other at home and then reflecting on what they experienced.

  3. Try creating variations on this exercise. For example, you might create a list of words (similar to what Freud might use with free association or Jung with the word-association test) and use them as trigger words. Or, you could have clients create their own lists of words.

Exercise

This exercise is to help you learn more about the effects of language on thinking, emotion, and our physiological states. Words can affect how we view the world and think about ourselves, and they can bring about negative physical experiences, such as heaviness in the body, tiredness, and even somatic sensations (for example, stomach upset, body tension). Others can lead to feeling physically stronger and experiencing increases in energy. By increasing our awareness, we can take better care in not just choosing our words but also in how we say them. To complete this exercise, please complete Parts I and II and the questions that follow.

Part I

  1. *Slowly repeat the following words aloud:*

    Sad. Helpless. Inconvenienced. Bored. Defeated. Tired. Lonely. Doubtful. Uninterested.

  2. *Next, read the following statements aloud:*

    Life is so hard. Nothing seems to go my way. There is no one to turn to or count on. It feels like I've been forgotten. Times are tough. Nothing seems to help. Things will not get better. In fact, they will probably get worse. There is no hope.

  3. Take a moment to write down what you are thinking, feeling, and sensing (physically).

_____

_____

_____

  4. Now consider what the specific words you repeated and experienced physiologically mean to you. In other words, what comes to mind when you study them?

_____

_____

_____

Part II

1. *Slowly repeat the following words aloud:*

   Exciting. Fun. Laughter. Joy. Anticipation. Attractive. Possibility. Aliveness. Peace. Love.

2. *Next, read the following statements aloud:*

   When I think about the future I become excited. I'm energized. There is so much I can accomplish. Life is wonderful and there are so many possibilities in the world.

3. Take a moment to write down what you are thinking, feeling, and sensing (physically).

   _____

   _____

   _____

4. Now consider what the specific words you repeated and experienced physiologically mean to you. In other words, what comes to mind when you study them?

   _____

   _____

   _____

Questions

1. What did you notice when you compared what you felt in your body physiologically in Part I with what you felt in Part II?

   _____

   _____

   _____

2. What did you notice when you compared what you thought in Part I with what you thought in Part II?

   _____

   _____

   _____

3. How might this be helpful to you?

_____

_____

_____

I.11   *What Are Words For? Terminology as a Pathway of Connection*

Therapist's Overview

Purpose of the Exercise

Attending to an individual's language is a subtle way to strengthen the therapeutic relationship. Paying attention to word choice and how clients perceive and label the role of the helper and helping process can go a long way in identifying client preferences. Matching language used during helping processes illustrates a willingness of the counselor to view the complaint from the client's world.

The purpose of this exercise is to discuss current terminology and determine the client's preferred language. Doing this in early sessions or interactions in the counseling process sets the stage for clear communication that can contribute to a positive outcome. This type of exercise is useful when clinicians are actively engaging clients in discussion about their preferred terminology and preferences. It is also helpful when working with individuals who are culturally different than the therapist.

Suggestions for Use

1. This exercise is written for adolescents and adults, although it can be modified to meet the developmental needs of children.
2. The purpose is to provide a better opportunity to identify client-preferred language.
3. Talk with clients about the words they use to describe change.

Exercise

To complete this exercise, ask the client to respond to a few of the following words as a means of learning more about his or her preferences in terminology.

Word		**Client Response**
Counseling	→	_____
Therapy	→	_____
Psychotherapy	→	_____
Psychoanalysis	→	_____
Couples Counseling	→	_____
Marriage Therapy	→	_____
Patient	→	_____
Client	→	_____
Therapist	→	_____
Counselor	→	_____
Change	→	_____
Growth	→	_____

Word		**Client Response**
Facilitate	→	_____
Strength	→	_____
Collaborate	→	_____
Healer	→	_____
Shaman	→	_____
Minister	→	_____
Coach	→	_____
Problem	→	_____
Empower	→	_____
Treat	→	_____
Diagnose	→	_____

After discussing the meaning of applicable words, ask the following questions of the client:

1. Which word(s) give you even the slightest sense that change is in your control?

_____

_____

2. When you have a sense of control over your complaint, what words describe that feeling?

_____

_____

3. When you talk about change, what words do you use?

_____

_____

4. What are possible benefits of talking about change in those terms?

_____

_____

5. How do these words give you a sense of hope?

_____

_____

_____

6. When you have a sense of positive change in your life, what words would you use to describe your experience?

_____

_____

By incorporating client responses, you accommodate his or her preferences and strengthen the therapeutic relationship.

I.12   Individuality, Uniqueness, and Strength: Working With People Who Have a Long List of Labels

Therapist's Overview

Purpose of the Exercise

Have you ever worked with an individual who has been going to counseling for years and can recite every diagnosis and medication given in his or her past? Perhaps this person has seen counselors, therapists, psychologists, psychiatrists, and social workers, each with a different perspective and treatment model. From past experience, this individual may have a strong knowledge of the *Diagnostic and Statistical Manual of Mental Disorders (DSM;* American Psychiatric Association) and the helping profession. Or perhaps as a result of his or her multiple counseling experiences, this person has become skeptical or resigned that the only thing that will ever change is his or her medication or diagnosis. The purpose of this exercise is to collaborate with your client by capitalizing on the client's knowledge and gaining from their experience to create positive, lasting change.

Suggestions for Use

1. This exercise is ideally suited for older adolescents and adults who have been working with helping professionals.
2. This exercise may also be beneficial when working with other health care professionals.
3. Utilizing this exercise early on in the therapeutic relationship could be most appropriate.

Exercise

Ideally, beginning this exercise during the intake or client history may strengthen the therapeutic relationship. After you have gathered your client's background information and discussed informed choice, consent, and the counseling process, ask your client, "When you have worked with other professionals what has worked best?" A simple follow-up question could be "How do you think that can be duplicated here?"

Here are some additional questions:

1. If you were the therapist and counseling yourself, how would you assess your readiness for change?

_____

_____

2. How could you take your knowledge of your readiness to change and amplify it just a bit?

_____

_____

3. What homework assignment would you give to yourself?

_____

_____

4. How would you assess if you were successful in completing your homework?

_____

_____

5. If you were the counselor, what do you think is most important to creating change?

_____

_____

6. When you hear your label or diagnosis, what feeling does it invoke?

_____

_____

7. If you wanted to increase or decrease that feeling, what is one thing you could do to accomplish your goal?

_____

_____

8. If you were to use your label or diagnosis with another person, how would you expect that person to respond?

_____

_____

9. When you think of your label or diagnosis, how do you make it "fit" into your definition of self?

_____

_____

10. What would it take to increase those positive feelings about yourself?

_____

_____

When in doubt about a particular course of action to take during a session, ask your client how counseling is going. It is a good way to stay both process and outcome informed.

I.13   Becoming the Hero of Your Own Story: Changing Narratives and Lives Through a Creative Process

Therapist's Overview

Purpose of the Exercise

Sometimes individuals and families can become so mired and overwhelmed in the circumstances of their lives that they have difficulty identifying any other more hopeful possibilities. Other clients have experiences that they find too painful to address directly. These clients may have forgotten that they are the heroes of their own lives and the champions of their own stories. It can be helpful during these times to provide these clients with an avenue to explore their situations from a safer distance.

This exercise is designed to assist therapists and clients in engaging in a collaborative process that promotes discussion and investigation on both metaphoric and literal levels. Before utilizing this exercise, therapists should first consider their own comfort with creativity and also the orientation of the individual with whom they are working. An adult, child, or youth with a strong sense of playfulness and with strong verbal skills is ideal for this activity.

Suggestions for Use

1. This exercise is helpful with parents, adolescents, children, and families who seem to be repeating the same story over and over.
2. Therapists should keep their responses and participation in the story within the milieu and characters established by the client. Try not to break the metaphor unless the client does so first.
3. Trust the process. This is an experiential activity that can produce information and insight that is surprising to all involved. What may seem irrelevant or nonsensical may be profoundly important to the client.
4. Allow ample time for the completion of this exercise. As always, allow the client to communicate when the story has reached its conclusion.

Exercise

When watching a movie, reading a book, or seeing a play, it can be enticing to imagine ourselves as the central character. In our minds we can slay the dragon, triumph over tragedy, or win the big game on a last-second shot. The power of story has been recognized for as long as there have been drawings in caves and gatherings around campfires. This exercise taps into this tradition to gently challenge our clients to view themselves as the principal and most powerful agents of change in their own stories. It may also help them see their situations from a slightly different point of view.

To begin, explain to the client that you will be creating a story together. You will ask the individual a few basic questions to get started, and then you will each take turns writing down a single line of the story on a piece of paper. As the story unfolds, the therapist should focus, in their narrative sentences, on the main character's strengths and successes. This interchange will continue until the client decides that the story is complete. Although the story may at first seem to have little to do with the client's circumstances, often it quickly becomes apparent that the client is writing a story about himself or herself. If old patterns and assumptions begin showing up in the narrative, gently challenge them, but always in the context established by the client.

Initial Questions

1. What is the title of the story?

2. Who is the main character?

3. What are the strengths of the main character? What does the main character do well?

4. What does the main character want?

5. Where does the story take place?

After collecting this information, begin writing the story.

Examples

CLIENT: Once there was a giant named Milo who was strong, smart, and a good cook.
THERAPIST: Milo lived in the woods at the top of a tall, cold mountain.
CLIENT: Milo was all alone in the world and had nobody to talk to.
THERAPIST: So he decided to go into town to use his strength and mind to find a friend.

CLIENT: Leslie ran from the wizard and hid under a rock.
THERAPIST: Then she remembered what she had to do to defeat him.
CLIENT: Leslie looked at the wizard and shook in fear.
THERAPIST: But she decided to stand up from under the rock and face him.

Concluding Questions

1. What would you like to add to our story?

2. What would you like to say about our story?

3. What successes did the main character have?

4. How did the main character change during the story?

_____

5. What do you think the main character will do differently next time?

_____

If clients choose to make direct literal connections to their lives, continue on that course of dialogue. If not, respect the integrity of the story and move on. For clients who enjoy and find benefit in this process, characters and stories can be revisited time and again.

SECTION II

GETTING FOCUSED
Exploring Strengths and Solutions in Information Gathering

II.1   *It Is Your Life: Creating Space for the Client's Story*

Therapist's Overview

Purpose of the Exercise

Therapy involves careful attention to clients' experiences, situations, concerns, and hopes for desired change. The primary doorways into clients' lives are their stories. It is therefore essential that therapists create "listening space"—contexts in which clients feel comfortable about the details associated with their coming to therapy. The unfolding of clients' stories or narratives is not only essential for therapists, but it will also be the most important part of therapy for some clients. In creating listening space, therapists let clients dictate the direction of opening conversations. Clients are invited to speak openly about only what they feel most comfortable. This allows clients to engage in dialogues that highlight both *what* they would like to talk about and *how* they would like to go about talking about it. The purpose of this exercise is to explore questions that invite clients to share their stories, particularly in the opening moments of therapy.

Suggestions for Use

1. This exercise is primarily for therapists as a way of exploring opening questions and continuing to reexamine them.
2. This exercise can be modified for use with clients. For example, clients could be asked to make a list of questions that they would consider respectful and helpful during opening and subsequent interactions.

Exercise

Many therapy approaches involve the use of opening questions aimed at steering therapy in a particular direction. This is a concern with both problem- and solution-focused approaches. Examples include the following: "What problem are you facing?" "What would you like to see change?" and "What has been going well in your life?" A concern with these types of questions is that they privilege the therapist's model and do not allow clients to start where they want and talk about what they want to talk about. A strengths-based approach is founded on the idea that clients ought to have the space to begin where they feel most comfortable. This creates a context in which clients can convey their stories in ways that are right for them. This, in turn, can strengthen the therapeutic relationship. To complete this exercise, please answer the questions below and write your answers in the spaces provided.

A strengths and solution-based (SSB) approach offers flexibility to therapists in terms of opening questions. Consider the following possibilities:

- Where would you like to start?
- What would you like to talk about?
- What is most important for me to know about you and your situation or concern?
- Are there certain things that you want to be sure we talk about?
- What do you want to be sure that we discuss during our time together?
- What ideas do you have about how therapy and coming to see me might be helpful?
- In what ways do you see me as being helpful to you in reaching your goals or achieving the change you desire?
- What do you feel or think you need from me right now?

- How can I be helpful to you right now?
- What do you see as my role in helping you with your concern?
- What, in your estimation, do therapists who are helpful do with their clients?

1. What did you notice about the questions listed?

_____

_____

_____

_____

2. What do they have in common?

_____

_____

_____

3. Which questions resonate most with you? Why?

_____

_____

_____

4. Generate a list of new questions that you might use in therapy.

1. _____

2. _____

3. _____

4. _____

5. _____

Consider that clients will need the space to start where they want in subsequent sessions as well. By creating listening space, we are conveying to clients that their preferences instead of therapists' theories are most important.

Next, consider implementing any of the questions listed in this exercise as part of your therapeutic work or in practice interactions.

II.2   *Hello, My Name Is: Meeting Yourself Again*

Therapist's Overview

Purpose of the Exercise

Change requires a reexamination of self and a new understanding of the changes made. This reexamination of the self and the change process can lead to ambivalence and ambiguity. Perhaps, for the fist time, clients are truly getting to know themselves. Working with your clients on this ambivalence and ambiguity and ultimately on their new self will go a long way to sustaining change.

The purpose of this exercise is for clients to relearn who they are and get a better understanding of their possible ambivalence and ambiguity centering on their change process. Many times clients have discussed with me their disappointment in their life because they are at a certain age and not where they believe they should be (for example, I am 42 years old and living at home again). A secondary aim of this exercise is to have clients value themselves for the stage of life they are in and not compare themselves to external factors of self-worth. One way to accomplish this task is to work with your clients on valuing their abilities and reducing their emphasis on past concerns.

Suggestions for Use

1. This exercise could be useful early on in the counseling process as a means to identify client strengths.
2. This exercise can be used as a tool to identify and capitalize on behavior used to meet client goals.
3. It can be used to allow for an opportunity to explore affect and emotion of your client's new self.
4. This exercise can be used in conjunction with Exercise II.18, "Embracing Your State: A Race with Yourself" and Exercise VI.6, "Giving Credit to Yourself: A New Look in the Mirror."

Exercise

Conceivably, you can begin this exercise during your first meeting when gathering background information. Discussing client resources is a useful conversation that will direct the conversation toward assets and strengths and away from negativity or deficits.

The following questions can be asked to facilitate change in a client's cognitive, affective, and behavioral understanding of self.

1. What is the number one quality that you like most about yourself?

_____

_____

2. How could you use that quality to improve your situation just a little bit?

_____

_____

3. What quality do you have that you would like to develop?

_____

_____

4. What would (insert an important person) see in you that would let him or her know you are developing that quality?

_____

_____

5. What needs to happen for you to increase the qualities you like most about yourself?

_____

_____

6. If you had to name or label your "new" self, what would it be?

_____

_____

7. What would (an important person) say was your new title to describe your life?

_____

_____

8. Describe how you value your strengths differently now that you have made these changes.

_____

_____

When an individual refers to himself or herself as his or her diagnosis, this exercise can be utilized as a means to shift that person's self identity away from pathology and toward strengths.

II.3   Lowering Walls and Building Bridges: Initial Steps in Creating Collaborative Relationships

Therapist's Overview

Purpose of the Exercise

The therapeutic milieu can, to some, seem like an artificial structure. Initially, clients are expected to share their concerns and struggles with someone who is, in all likelihood, nearly a complete stranger. On the opposite side of the coin, therapists may fall into the trap of quickly assessing and advising a client without fully understanding or taking into account the totality of the person. This exercise is intended to, in part, ameliorate the potential awkwardness of first interactions as well as to level any perceived power differential on the part of the client. It also emphasizes core SSB premises of a strong focus on humanism and the importance of relationships. As a caution, therapists should take much care if discussing one's own overly personal information during the course of this activity.

Suggestions for Use

1. This exercise is intended for utilization during the first session and particularly with clients who have never participated in therapy.
2. As with all exercises, the client has the right to decline to answer any and all questions and should not be pressed for elaboration of answers beyond brief, gentle follow-up.
3. Cross-reference: This exercise may be used as a companion to Exercise I.9, "Expectations and Next-Pectations: Learning Clients' Preferences for Therapy."

Exercise

If you have ever been stuck at a party talking to a complete stranger, you know how difficult first conversations can be. "What do I say?" "Can I just be myself?" "Who is this person I am talking to?" Some people experience the first session of therapy in much the same way. As we begin our work together, it is important that we each have some understanding of the person sitting across from the other. To be sure, there is more to every person than can be described by a simple activity, but the following exercise is intended to provide you with an opportunity to share a little more about yourself than just what brought you here today. At the same time, it is hoped it will also give you a bit of insight into the person with whom you are beginning to work. Below you will find several sentence stems. Simply fill in the blanks in any way that makes sense to you and I will do the same. When we finish, we can either discuss our responses verbally or trade worksheets, whatever is most comfortable to you. Feel free to make your answers as long or short as you would like.

1. My name is _____ .

2. I am a _____ .

3. I like to _____ .

4. I think about _____ .

5. I feel happiest when _____ .

6. Others say I _____ .

7. I wish _____ .

8. My life would be better if _____ .

9. When I am alone I _____ .

10. I worry about _____ .

11. In the future _____ .

12. A perfect day is _____ .

13. My family _____ .

14. I wish people knew _____ .

II.4   Stone Soup: Acknowledging Strengths, Potential, and Contributions to Change

Therapist's Overview

Purpose of the Exercise

Sometimes families initiate services with rigid ideas about themselves and as individual members of the unit. Although some clinicians conceptualize each family member as unique contributors to a problem, strengths-based helpers see just the opposite. This exercise is meant to facilitate a discussion that explores the various manners in which individuals in a family system can be active players in the therapeutic process. The dialogue that ensues from the activity can help the clinician and the family to discover greater commonality of goals as well as a clearer understanding of possible pathways to achieve those goals.

Suggestions for Use

1. This exercise is intended for use with families and groups toward the beginning of the process to facilitate assessment and goal setting.
2. It is helpful to have available something on which to write each response en masse so that the sum total may be observed at the conclusion of the exercise.
3. Each individual family member should have a copy of the below worksheet on which to record responses.

Exercise

Every family and group has its own unique set of traits and personalities. Like the old story of stone soup, everyone contributes something individual to the pot that, together, creates something different and perhaps greater than the individual parts. When families struggle, it can be easy for members to begin focusing on what is spoiling the soup rather than on what is enhancing its flavor. Please take a few moments to write below what you think you bring that enhances your family unit. It may be a sense of humor, organization, pride, among many other possibilities. After you name your contributions, please write down what other members of your family do to make your soup better.

My Name

_____

What I Bring:

_____

_____

Family Member #1

_____

What He/She Brings:

_____

_____

Family Member #2

_____

What He/She Brings:

_____

_____

Family Member #3

_____

What He/She Brings:

_____

_____

Family Member #4

_____

What He/She Brings:

_____

_____

Family Member #5

_____

What He/She Brings:

_____

_____

Family Member #6

_____

What He/She Brings:

_____

_____

Now I would like for us to go around the room and have each of you take turns telling us what you wrote about yourselves. After that, each of you will choose another family member to say what he or she wrote about you. I will write down all of the responses.

After everyone has had an opportunity to share, write your responses to the following questions.

1. What do you notice about your family's soup? What, if any, questions do you have about it?

_____

_____

_____

_____

2. How can the ingredients of your soup help your family reach its goals?

_____

_____

_____

3. How will your individual ingredient help your family reach its goal?

_____

_____

_____

II.5   Stenographer: I Said What?

Therapist's Overview

Purpose of the Exercise

It is common practice in many graduate programs for therapists in training to in some way record either mock or actual sessions. The act of getting out of one's head and paying attention to choice of words, body language, and content provides perspective not available while in the throes of a conversation. With this exercise, clients can have a variation on the same experience. By clearly and accurately recording and repeating a client's words, the therapist can facilitate for the client the experience of hearing their concern from a safe distance. It is also a form of role play that places clients in the position of giving themselves advice. This allows the therapist to hear from the client examples of the types of questions and advice that are most helpful to them.

Suggestions for Use

1. This activity can be used at any time during the process with individual clients.
2. The therapist should take care not to add anything to that which the client initially offers.
3. Cross-references: This exercise can be used in conjunction with Exercise IV.12, "Vantage Point: Multiple Angles, Multiple Solutions," and Exercise I.9, "Expectations and Next-Pectations: Learning Clients' Preferences for Therapy."

Exercise

The mind can be a lonely place. When life becomes overwhelming, it is easy for some people to retreat within themselves. This may sometimes be helpful, but at other times, runaway thoughts and worries take over and become paralyzing. This activity is intended provide you with space to listen to your concerns from a distance sufficient enough to make them more manageable. While playing the role of therapist, you will be asked to ask questions and generate advice for someone in your situation.

To begin, please fill out the following.

1. Please describe your primary concern today.

_____

_____

_____

2. How long has this concern been present?

_____

_____

_____

3. What have you tried in the past to address the issue?

_____

_____

_____

_____

4. How successful was that strategy?

_____

_____

_____

_____

Next, please give your responses to your therapist. You will now reverse roles. Please read from the suggested questions and statements below. Your therapist will respond using the answers you provided. Please record those responses in the spaces provided.

1. Please describe what brings you in today.

_____

_____

_____

2. How long has this been going on and what have you tried in the past to address it?

_____

_____

_____

3. The following is a suggestion that may be helpful to you.

_____

_____

_____

4. When others have been in your situation, this is something they often want to hear.

_____

_____

_____

_____

5. I wonder if you have thought about the following:

_____

_____

_____

_____

6. My best piece of advice to you is:

_____

_____

_____

_____

It may now be helpful to consider the following questions:

1. Was there anything about the exercise that you found surprising?

2. Were there any other questions or statements you wanted to ask as the therapist?

3. What was your experience hearing your words recited back to you?

4. What did you learn about your situation?

5. If you were to do this again, would you add anything to your initial description of your situation?

II.6   *What Is the Effect? Exploring the Influences of Problems*

Therapist's Overview

Purpose of the Exercise

The essence of problems is that they somehow have negative effects on people and their lives. This is important because there are concerns that people may have that they do not like but nonetheless live with. These concerns may not significantly impact well-being, relationships, and social functioning. A task of therapists is to develop a clear understanding of how problems have or are currently disrupting people's everyday functioning and then collaborate with clients on goals and tasks to accomplish those goals. The purpose of this exercise is to establish clarity by asking questions to explore the ways in which problems affect people's lives.

Suggestions for Use

1. This exercise can be used at different points in therapy but is particularly applicable at the beginning of therapy.
2. This exercise can be completed with clients or can be given to them to complete on their own. It can also be used to generate questions in therapy.
3. Cross-reference: See Exercise II.1, "It Is Your Life: Creating Space for the Client's Story."

Exercise

There are things that happen in our lives that we might consider nuisances and would like to go away; however, not all of these things are necessarily problems in the sense that they have a negative effect on our lives. This exercise is to bring clarity to therapy by further elaborating on what we consider "problems" by exploring the impact that our concerns have on our individual well-being, relationships, and social life (i.e., work, school, friendships, etc.). The clearer we are on how the concerns we have negatively impact us, the more specific we can be in coming up with ways of addressing them. To complete this exercise, please write your responses in the spaces provided.

Briefly describe the most significant concern you are currently experiencing (or, if you are seeing a therapist, what brought you to therapy).

_____

_____

_____

_____

Consider how the primary concern you described above has negatively impacted your life. Now, describe the problem's effects on the following areas:

1. Personal Well-Being (i.e., how the problem has affected you, including your self-esteem and sense of self)

_____

_____

_____

2. Close Relationships (i.e., intimate relationships, family, very close friends)

_____

_____

_____

_____

3. Social (i.e., job, school, other friendships, community activity)

_____

_____

_____

_____

Take a moment to review your responses. What stands out for you? What, if anything, is clearer to you as a result?

_____

_____

_____

_____

II.7   What Does That Look Like? Translating Ambiguity Through Action-Talk

Therapist's Overview

Purpose of Exercise

One of the ways we can increase the chance for success in therapy is by gaining clarity about what needs to change. Because people will often describe their concerns in vague, nondescriptive terms, it is up to therapists to ask questions for clarification. Lack of clarity can lead to frustration, labeling clients as resistant or unmotivated, misguided selection of methods, and so on. Clear descriptions, however, can assist therapists with targeting specific concerns, choosing methods that are a good fit, and increasing the expectations for positive change. The purpose of this exercise is to use "action-talk" to clarify problems and concerns. Action-talk allows for therapists, clients, and others who may be involved to gain clear, behavioral descriptions.

Suggestions for Use

1. Give examples of changing vague, nondescriptive translations into clear, observable, behavioral descriptions by using action-talk.
2. Discuss how vague descriptions can lead to unhelpful or misguided attempts at solving problems and finding solutions.
3. Once clients have used action-talk, ask them what new ideas they might have about how to deal with their concern(s).
4. This exercise can be used at any point in therapy where clients are using vague, nondescriptive words. It can also be helpful to therapists when there is a lack of clarity regarding the focus of therapy.
5. Encourage clients to proceed to Exercise II.8, "G-O! Focusing on Goals and Outcomes" following the completion of this exercise.
6. Cross-references: Exercise II.8, "G-O! Focusing on Goals and Outcomes" and Exercise II.9, "Goals for Goal Setting."

Exercise

The clearer the concern and what needs to be different or changed, the more focused attempts can be to bring about that change. This exercise is to translate ambiguous or vague, nondescriptive language into clear observable actions through the use of "action-talk." Action-talk helps us to determine both the "doing" of problems and solutions. There are two parts to this exercise. In the first part we will practice clarifying concerns. In the second, focus will be on translating this process to the therapy setting.

To complete this exercise, please review the examples given. Next, write your responses to the prompts in the spaces provided.

Part I

First view the example sequences of moving from vague descriptions to action-talk descriptions. Notice that one example involves further clarifying questions to turn vague statements into clear, action-based ones.

EXAMPLE 1

Vague problem description → "My life is spinning out of control."
↓
   Clarifying question → "What specifically has happened to indicate to you that your life is spinning out of control?"
↓
   Action-talk description → "I haven't been able to make it to work on time in the past two weeks."

EXAMPLE 2

Vague problem description → "My anxiety is taking over."
↓
Clarifying question → "What have you noticed happening in your life recently that signals you that your anxiety is taking over?"
↓
Further vague problem description → "I feel panicked a lot."
↓
Further clarifying question → "What specifically happens when you feel panicked?"
↓
Action-talk description → "I lose my train of thought and get overwhelmed by thoughts."
↓
Further clarifying question → "What do you do when you are overwhelmed by your thoughts?"
↓
Action-talk description → "I get distracted and don't get the things I've set out to do done."

As indicated in Example 2, when client responses remain vague, it is sometimes necessary to ask a series of clarifying questions.

In this section, using action-talk, for each vague problem description write down a question that can be used to clarify and create a clear, action-based description.

Vague problem description → "I have a drinking problem."
↓
Clarifying question → " _____

_____ ?"

Vague problem description → "My son has an anger problem."
↓
Clarifying question → " _____

_____ ?"

Vague problem description → "I'm in a codependent relationship."
↓
Clarifying question → " _____

_____ ?"

Part II

Now let us translate this to your therapeutic work. Below, in the left-hand column, are a few examples of vague problem descriptions. Your goal is to write down vague problem descriptions you have heard from your clients. You can also choose to practice this with a partner in a role play. In the left-hand column below, list those concerns. Then, in the right-hand column, use action-talk to get a clearer picture of your complaint.

Problem Description   Action-Talk Description (if not clear in first column)

1. _____   →   _____

_____   →   _____

_____   →   _____

2. _____   →   _____

_____   →   _____

_____   →   _____

3. _____   →   _____

_____   →   _____

_____   →   _____

4. _____   →   _____

_____   →   _____

_____   →   _____

5. _____   →   _____

_____   →   _____

_____   →   _____

After completing this exercise, you are encouraged to complete Exercise II.8, "G-O! Focusing on Goals and Outcomes."

II.8   G-O! Focusing on Goals and Outcomes

Therapist's Overview

Purpose of the Exercise

It is common for therapists to confuse goals and outcomes and consider them the same. Although the two are intertwined, they are very different entities. *Goals* are concrete, behavioral descriptions of what clients want different in their lives. *Outcomes* represent clients' subjective interpretations of the impact of services on specific areas of clients' lives, including individual well-being, interpersonal relationships, and social roles. Both goals and outcomes are important in determining client change. Goals are important for helping clients to identify and target specific behavioral changes, and outcomes help to better understand client functioning. This is crucial to understand because achieving a goal does not necessarily correlate to an improved outcome. For example, a client can reach a goal of getting to work on time more often than not, but if he or she does not experience an improved sense of individual well-being, then the achievement of that particular goal may carry less meaning. The purpose of this exercise is to help practitioners to further distinguish between goals and outcomes (G-O) and begin to create ways of exploring both with clients.

Suggestions for Use

1. This exercise can be used by therapists to practice differentiating between goals and outcomes and in working with clients.
2. It is important to note that achieving a goal does not necessarily mean a client has experienced an improved outcome and vice versa. Transition into other forms of services or out of therapy should not occur exclusively on the basis of one or the other and should include client feedback.
3. Both goals and outcomes can change and should be revisited on a regular basis with clients.
4. Cross-reference: This exercise can be used in conjunction with Exercise II.7, "What Does That Look Like? Translating Ambiguity Through Action-Talk" and Exercise II.9, "Goals for Goal-Setting: Charting a Clear Course."

Exercise

Both goals and outcomes are important to successful therapy. Goals represent concrete depictions of specific behaviors that clients would like to have different in their lives; outcomes relate to clients' ratings of the impact of services in various areas of their lives. These generally include individual well-being, interpersonal relationships, and social roles. Goals are important because they help clients and therapists identify concrete, measurable behavioral changes. Outcomes are also important in that they help therapists to understand if and to what degree clients are reporting improvement in primary areas of their lives.

The purpose of this exercise is to help you to distinguish between goals and outcomes and explore how to orient therapy toward these two entities. To complete this exercise, please answer the questions in Parts I and II by writing your answers in the spaces provided.

Part I

The first part of the G-O equation is goals, which are concrete, behavioral changes that clients seek. Goals have certain characteristics. First, they describe what people want as opposed to what they do not—that is, what people seek instead of problems. Think of goals as those things that can be measured. For this part of the exercise, refer to the examples offered and write your responses in the places provided.

Examples of Goal Descriptions

- I would like to make it to work on time more often than not—at least 80% of the time.
- I want to be able to resolve my disagreements with my partner without us yelling at each other.
- I want to be able to relax when I have to take an exam for school.

Now review the ambiguous statements listed below. Notice that they are vague and reflect what clients do not want. Then write down two questions that you could ask to help clarify what is wanted instead of each concern.

1. Client Response: "I don't want to be overwhelmed by my thoughts."

    Clarifying Questions:

    a. _____

    b. _____

2. Client Response: "I'm tired of being late to work."

    Clarifying Questions:

    a. _____

    b. _____

3. Client Response: "I don't want to continue to be unappreciated by my boss."

    Clarifying Questions:

    a. _____

    b. _____

Next, for each of the items in the previous section, write down a possible goal that might result from the questions you wrote. Make sure that each goal is clear, action based, and describes what is wanted instead of what is not.

Goal Description for #1

_____

_____

Goal Description for #2

_____

_____

Goal Description for #3

_____

_____

Part II

The second part of the G-O equation is outcomes. As discussed, outcomes measure clients' subjective interpretations of the impact of services provided. This most often relates to some degree of change in their individual well-being or sense of self, such as a reduction of symptoms. Outcomes also include an emphasis on relationships, such as how well clients are getting along with others and the strength of their family support systems. A final area is social role that refers to how things are for clients in terms of employment, school, community, and so on. Outcomes are important because they indicate the level of distress clients are experiencing at a point in time. Because a client can achieve a goal without an improvement in outcome, we want to tune into ways that can help clients to experience not only concrete changes but also subjective ones that correlate with improved functioning in all aspects of their lives.

To complete this part of the exercise, consider specific areas that might give indication that your client is improving in major areas of his or her life. As a note, many outcome measures are negatively skewed and focus on the absence or diminishment of symptoms as criteria for improvement. Therefore, you will need to consider what will increase in clients' lives that suggests improvement. To do this, refer to the examples given on the left side of the paper, and on the right, write down possible indicators of an improved outcome.

INDIVIDUAL WELL-BEING

NEGATIVE SYMPTOM	IMPROVEMENT
Examples:	Examples:
Unsatisfied with life	*Satisfied with how things are going*
Lack of sleep	*Sleeping longer and feel better rested*
No interest	*Excited about things in life*
Blame Self	_____
Irritated	_____
Fearful	_____
Drugs	_____
Worthless	_____
Nervous	_____

INTERPERSONAL RELATIONSHIPS

NEGATIVE SYMPTOM	IMPROVEMENT

Examples:

Feel lonely and isolated

Argue with others

Examples:

Feel connection to others/have friends

Get along well with others

Strained Family Relationships

Trouble Getting Along With Close
  Acquaintances

_____

_____

Others Criticize My Drug/Drug Use

_____

SOCIAL ROLE

NEGATIVE SYMPTOM	IMPROVEMENT

Examples:

Stressed at work or school

Drinking/drugs interfere with work/school

Examples:

Feel relaxed/comfortable at school/work

Manage work/school without drugs

School or Work Is Unsatisfying

Not Accomplishing Work- or School-Related
  Activities

_____

_____

Uninvolved With Community

_____

Now, refer back to the goals you outlined in Part I. In the spaces below, write one or two possible indicators of an improved outcome for each goal.

Outcome Indicators for Goal #1

1. _____

2. _____

Outcome Indicators for Goal #2

1. _____

2. _____

Outcome Indicators for Goal #3

1. _____

2. _____

For further resources on outcome measurement instrumentation, please refer to the following:

Burlingame, G. B., Lambert, M. J., Reisinger, C. W., Neff, W. L., Mosier, J. (1995). Pragmatics of tracking mental health outcomes in a managed care setting. *The Journal of Mental Health Administration, 22*, 226–236.

Burlingame, G. B., Mosier, J. L., Wells, M. G., Atkin, Q. G., Lambert, M. J., & Whoolery, M. (2001). Tracking the influence of mental health outcome. *Clinical Psychology and Psychotherapy, 8*, 361–379.

Burlingame, G. B., Wells, M. G., & Lambert, M. J. (1996). *Youth Outcome Questionnaire*. Stevenson, MD: American Professional Credentialing Services.

Burlingame, G. B., Wells, M. G., Lambert M. J., & Cox, J. (2004). Youth Outcome Questionnaire: Updated psychometric properties. In M. E. Maruish (Ed.), *The use of psychological testing for treatment planning and outcome assessment* (3rd ed.). Mahwah, NJ: Lawrence Erlbaum.

Dunn, T. W., Burlingame, G. M., Walbridge, M., Smith, J., & Crum, M. J. (2005). Outcome assessment for children and adolescents: Psychometric validation of the Youth Outcome Questionnaire 30.1 (Y-OQ®-30.1). *Clinical Psychology and Psychotherapy, 12*, 388–401.

Lambert, M. J., & Burlingame, G. R. (1996). *Outcome Questionnaire 45.2*. Wilmington, Delaware: American Professional Credentialing Services.

Lambert, M. J., & Burlingame, G. R., Umphress, V., Hansen, N. B., Vermeersch, D. A., Clouse, G. C., & Yanchar, S. C. (1996). The reliability and validity of the Outcome Questionnaire. *Clinical Psychology, 3*(4), 249–258.

Lambert, M. J., & Finch, A. E. (1999). The Outcome Questionnaire. In M. E. Maruish (Ed.), *The use of psychological testing for treatment planning and outcome assessment* (2nd ed.). Mahwah, NJ: Lawrence Erlbaum.

Miller S. D., & Duncan, B. L. (2000). *The Outcome Rating Scale*. Chicago: Author.

Miller, S. D., Duncan, B. L., Brown, J. S., Sparks, J. A., Claud, D. A. (2003). The Outcome Rating Scale: A preliminary study of the reliability, validity, and feasibility of a brief, visual, analog measure. *Journal of Brief Therapy, 2*, 91–100.

II.9   *Goals for Goal Setting: Charting a Clear Course*

Therapist's Overview

Purpose of the Exercise

A central component to SSB therapy is the use of questioning techniques. Questions set the stage for individuals to cognitively engage in concrete terms to address their complaints. Goal setting is one technique that can produce focused attention on clients' needs.

The use of goal setting is not new to counseling; however, this exercise hopes to capitalize cognitive psychology and critical thinking to increase the benefit of goal setting. The foundation for this exercise comes from the Methods of Inquiry program (Ahuna & Tinnesz, 2006). Methods of Inquiry teaches individuals to become self-regulated learners by knowing individual strengths, weaknesses, and means to increase their ability to learn. This is an approach that parallels strength-based counseling.

Suggestions for Use

1. This exercise can be used with all individuals.
2. Goals can be used as a follow-up to a first-session task. Once a client notices how things are different, goals can be developed to sustain change.
3. This exercise could be useful for individuals who are analytic thinkers and those who may need encouragement to direct their thinking in a specific direction.

Exercise

When using goal setting in counseling, it may be beneficial to consider goals that are (a) specific and measurable, (b) realistic, (c) challenging, and (d) have a specific start and end date.

For example, if you were working with an individual contemplating a career change, the individual's goal setting may include determining a new career and searching out training programs (specific and measurable), having an aptitude for the new career (realistic), entering the training or schooling (challenging), and completing the training or schooling (specific start and end dates). When working with an individual with an involved or long-term goal, it may be helpful to break down the goal into two or more subgoals. Meeting many small goals in a short period of time can increase an individual's sense of self-efficacy in accomplishing his or her main goal.

Perhaps this goal sheet will help you collaborate with your client.

Goal: _____

   1. Describe how the goal is specific and measurable:

_____

_____

   2. Describe how the goal is realistic:

_____

_____

3. Describe how the goal is challenging:

_____

_____

4. Write the start and end dates of the goal:

_____

_____

5. Describe one or two subgoals that will lead to the accomplishment of the main goal:

_____

_____

Here are a few suggestions to think about during and after goal setting:

1. During the goal-setting process, capitalize on client strengths and resources.
2. In reviewing goals, amplify changes they have begun and look for further exceptions to client complaints.

Reference

Ahuna, K. H., & Tinnesz, C. G. (2006). *Methods of inquiry applied critical thinking* (2nd ed). Dubuque, IA: Kendall/Hunt.

II.10   From Problem-Talk to Solution-Talk: Creating Possibilities Through Language

Therapist's Overview

Purpose of the Exercise

It has been said that language is a virus. Words can be very influential—conveying pathology and problems or possibilities and solutions. One of the ways we can facilitate change is by paying close attention to how we use words and by considering how language plays a role in both the construction and resolution of problems. This serves several purposes. First, it focuses on the positive intent behind behavior, such as working toward meeting a need. Second, it assists with creating solvable problems. A third benefit is it can promote hope through language that is less stigmatizing and blaming. A fourth reason is that it can generate new possibilities and solutions while also addressing any concerns. By making changes in how we talk about clients' concerns, we can neutralize defensiveness, build rapport, and spawn creativity. The purpose of this exercise is to make changes in the basic language that is used when identifying what the concerns are with clients. This entails shifting from "problem-talk" to "solution-talk."

Suggestions for Use

1. This exercise can be completed by therapists as a way of thinking differently about concerns and possible solutions or with clients to generate new conversations for change.
2. If using with clients, it can be helpful to give examples of both problem-talk and solution-talk.
3. After completing this exercise, it may be helpful to consider what new ideas may have emerged about how to approach concerns as a result of using solution-talk.
4. Cross-reference: This exercise can be used in conjunction with Exercise I.10, "The Body Knows: The Influence of Words."

Exercise

"Problems" are, at least in part, socially constructed representations of what has been identified as going "wrong." Therapy certainly involves discussion of what is not working and how individuations, relationships, systems, and situations can change. The trouble with problem-talk is that it can stigmatize, blame, and demoralize; it frequently assumes negative intentions on the part of others; it very rarely defines problems in ways that are solvable; and it closes down possibilities for change. The antidote is solution-talk, which helps therapists and clients to redefine concerns in ways that assume the best intentions of others, contribute to the creation of solvable problems, and open up possibilities for solutions. It is important to note that we are not suggesting that therapists ignore problems and only talk about solutions. Instead we are advocating for conversations in which clients' concerns are both clearly presented and understood and that therapists, with clients, engage in conversations in which behaviors and actions are described in less blaming and stigmatizing ways. These types of conversations not only help with identifying the positive intentions behind the behavior and how actions may be attempts to meet needs, they move conversations toward solutions and possibilities. The purpose of this exercise is to encourage solution-talk as a path to change.

To complete this exercise, please refer to the problem-talk descriptions listed in the left column and fill in the blank in the corresponding right column by using solution-talk. Examples have been provided to assist you.

PROBLEM-TALK	SOLUTION-TALK
Isolates	Is introspective and thoughtful
Resistant	Is careful to do what is best for self
Manipulative	Good at getting needs met
Anger problem	Gets upset sometimes
Disobedient	_____
Rebellious	_____
Disruptive	_____
Disrespectful	_____
Enmeshed	_____
Disconnected	_____

In addition to more general problem-talk, diagnostic language can contribute to conversations that unnecessarily stigmatize, blame, and close down possibilities for change. In this next section, please locate the diagnostic, problem-talk description in the left column and write down a corresponding solution-talk description in the corresponding right column.

ADHD	Very energetic; is *sometimes* easily distracted
Bipolar	Experiences significant ups and downs
Dissociative	Protects self emotionally when threatened
Manic	_____
Major Depressive	_____
Reactive Attachment	_____
Obsessive-Compulsive	_____
Oppositional/Defiant	_____
Antisocial	_____

Next, in the left-hand column write down some common problem-focused descriptions you are familiar with and change them to solution-talk. Please write your responses in the right-hand column.

_____	_____
_____	_____
_____	_____
_____	_____
_____	_____
_____	_____

For this final part, please complete the following questions.

1. What did you learn by changing the problem-focused terms to solution-talk?

_____

_____

_____

_____

2. What ideas do you have for introducing solution-talk when conversations turn negative and laden with problem-talk?

_____

_____

_____

_____

It is crucial to keep in mind that therapeutic conversations involve both problem-talk and solution-talk. It is not an "either/or" proposition. In addition, we do not minimize the problems that people experience, nor do we simply try to be positive and "spin" problems into a positive light. What is clear is that problem-talk can have a host of very negative consequences for both clients and therapists. By working with clients to identify their concerns and then introduce new ways of talking about those concerns through solution-talk, we see people as capable and their behavior as their best attempts to get their needs met. This can help us to think differently about the concerns presented and to generate new possibilities for solutions that otherwise would be unavailable through problem-talk.

II.11   Future Screening: Creating a Vision for the Future

Therapist's Overview

Purpose of the Exercise

There are sayings, "If you don't know where you're going you probably end up somewhere else" and "If you don't know where you're going you'll probably end up there." A lack of direction can not only be a path to unsuccessful therapy, it can contribute to frustration, anxiety, confusion, and diminished hope on the part of both therapists and clients. This makes it essential that all persons involved in the therapeutic milieu know what is trying to be accomplished.

One of the ways to gain clarity regarding direction is to create a sense of the future through a "Future Screening." The purpose of this exercise is to assist clients in picturing what their futures will look like when the problems for which they have sought help are resolved. When it is clear what clients want different in their lives and situations, we can work backward to help them take steps to achieve those desired visions—hence, changes. Clarity about concerns can assist with the development of methods (tasks to achieve goals and change) that provide a better fit for clients.

This exercise can be used at any point where focus is needed, particularly in determining what needs to change or be different for clients. It can be used at the start of services, in conjunction with establishing goals, or at any juncture when goals have been modified or changed altogether.

Suggestions for Use

1. Familiarize clients with "action-talk."
2. There are times when clients will create visions of the future that appear unattainable or unrealistic. It is important to acknowledge their viewpoints and work to further shape those visions to determine which aspects clients can work on in the present or immediate future. For example, if a client's vision were to have a parent back who passed away, the therapist might inquire as to what difference that would make for the client. From this, the therapist learns that the client felt understood by her parent. The therapist could then help the client to explore her life for, or how to develop, other relationships in which she could feel understood more often than she is currently. The aim is to determine not only what clients want different in their futures, but what that difference symbolizes for them.
3. Although some clients will develop more elaborate visions, it is not necessary. Work to help clients develop a vision of some aspect of their future where things are going better. This could mean complete problem resolution or a reduction of the intensity or severity of concerns such that their lives are improved.
4. This exercise can be used with adults, adolescents, or children. It can also be used as part of individual, family, couples, or group therapy. For younger clients, it may be helpful to be creative by having them draw images or pictures of their vision-quests.
5. Cross-reference: This activity involves the use of "action-talk." To learn about this, please refer to the activity presented in Exercise II.7, "What Does That Look Like? Translating Ambiguity Through Action-Talk."

Exercise

Have you ever tried to figure out where to start with a problem you are facing? Sometimes it can be overwhelming. This exercise will help you to find a starting point by identifying what your situation or life will look like when the problem you are facing is either no longer a problem or the negative effects of it have been significantly reduced. With this vision you can then work to make it a reality. This exercise requires you to exercise your imagination just a bit. Are you ready?

To complete this exercise, please do the following:

1. Choose a wall, the floor, or a part of the sky that is devoid of objects and could serve as a screen—an area on which you could see images superimposed. Next, imagine that you have a fast-forward button at your fingertips. You can use this button when you want and at whatever rate of speed you want.

   Imagine your life as a movie that is now playing on your screen. When you reach a point that you feel symbolizes how things are for you, freeze that image. On a scale of 1 to 10, with 1 being the worst your life could be and 10 being the best it could be, how would you rate things? Please write your initial rating in the space provided below and provide any associated feelings and thoughts.

Initial Rating: _____

   a. Please list any thoughts and feelings or sensations you are having that are associated with this image:

   _____

   _____

   _____

2. Next, take a deep breath. Now use the fast-forward button to move your life screenplay forward in such a way that the image becomes blurry. You can choose to move the image quickly or slowly, but make sure that it is out of focus. (You can choose to close your eyes during this part if it is easier for you.) As your screenplay progresses, take a deep breath and consider that your life story is changing. The problem that you have been grappling with is being resolved as the screening moves on and on.

   Stay with it just a few more seconds. Now, consider that the problem that had once been so dominating is no longer affecting your life as it once had. In fact, it is either completely gone or barely noticeable. When you are ready, hit the "stop" button. Focus the image so it is clear. Then, answer the questions that follow.

   a. How far into the future are you?

   _____

   _____

   b. What is happening?

   _____

   _____

    c. How was the problem you once experienced resolved?

_____

_____

  3. What is your current rating (on a scale of 1 to 10)?

    a. Please list any thoughts and feelings or sensations you are having that are associated with this image:

_____

_____

  4. For this final part, in the spaces provided below, write down three things that you could do right now or in the next few days, weeks, or months to begin to move toward the future that you envisioned, to begin to make it a reality.

    a. _____

_____

    b, _____

_____

    c. _____

_____

II.12 Destination Imagination: Envisioning the Future Through Miracles, Dreams, and the Extraterrestrial

Therapist's Overview

Purpose of the Exercise

An integral part of therapy is helping clients to develop a clear sense of what they would like to have change or be different in their lives. This involves helping them to create a vision of the future where the problems that brought them to therapy have been resolved or at least become more manageable. By gaining a vision of the future in which things are going better for clients, we can help them to work backwards to bring those visions to life. To assist with developing an improved sense of the future, it can sometimes be helpful to use methods that encourage creativity on the part of clients. This helps to engage clients, such as children and adolescents, and to introduce new ways of thinking about the future. The purpose of this exercise is to explore several specific methods that are all aimed at helping clients to develop and articulate what they would like to have happen in the future that would indicate improvement over their current situations. This can bring clarity to both clients and therapists through the identification of a unified direction.

As a reminder, because this exercise involves the use of specific methods, some will not be a good fit with some clients. It is up to the therapist to work closely with each client, carefully considering which methods offer the best options for fit. If a particular method does not work, the therapist should abandon it and move on. It is not the technique that is important. What is important is helping clients articulate what they would like to see their lives like "down the road" when their situations are improved and the problems that brought them to therapy have been resolved or have dissipated. As an alternative, for those clients who may respond more to straightforward future-focused questions, refer to the exercise in Exercise II.13, "I Can See Clearly Now: Developing a Future Focus."

Suggestions for Use

1. This exercise can be completed by therapists as a way of thinking differently about concerns and possible solutions or with clients to generate new conversations for change.
2. In helping clients to create or rehabilitate their visions for the future, it is important to make sure that what clients want is realistic and attainable.
3. For some clients, it can be helpful to identify smaller steps toward their overall vision of the future.
4. Some clients may struggle with a certain method. It is important to remain flexible and keep in mind the overall intent of using the methods outlined. The methods are a means of assisting clients with creating a vision of the future. There are many ways of doing this, and some methods will be a better fit for some clients.
5. Cross-references: This exercise can be used in conjunction with Exercise II.11, "Future Screening: Creating a Vision for the Future" and Exercise II.13, "I Can See Clearly Now: Developing a Future Focus."

Exercise

There is the saying, "If you don't know where you're going you'll probably end up somewhere else." This speaks to the importance of working with clients to determine what they would like to see or have different in their lives. To do this, this goal of this exercise is to help to envision and articulate a view of the future in which the problems that your clients have brought to therapy are resolved or are at least manageable. To do this, we will explore a few creative techniques for assisting with this process. To complete this exercise, please complete Parts I and II by following the directions below and placing your answers in the spaces provided.

Part I

Please choose one of the following methods below and answer the associated questions. Next, proceed to Part II to complete the second part of the exercise.

The Crystal Ball

Imagine that you have a crystal ball and you can peer into the past, the present, and the future. Now focus on the crystal ball that represents the future.

　1. What do you see?

_____

_____

　2. Notice that you can see your future. You can look a few days, months, or years, whatever makes sense for you. When you are ready, go to a time in the future when things are going better for you. What is happening?

_____

_____

　3. Notice that the problem you had in the past that brought you to therapy has gone away. What happened?

_____

_____

Miracles

Suppose that tonight, while you were sleeping, a miracle happened. The miracle is that the problem that brought you to therapy has vanished completely.

　1. What would be the first thing you noticed when you woke up that would tell you a miracle happened?

_____

_____

　2. What would be different?

_____

_____

The Dreamer

Let us say that last night or a few nights ago you had a wonderful dream about the future. In this dream you experienced a change of events in which the concern that lead you to see me has disappeared and gone away. Take a moment to think about that. Now, suppose that you can remember a little about that dream you had and can tell me about it. It may come to you slowly or quickly.

　　1. What happened?

_____

_____

　　2. What changed?

_____

_____

The Time Machine

Let us say there is a time machine sitting here in the office. Let us say that you climb in and it propels you into the future, to a time when things are going the way you want them to go. After arriving at your future destination, the first thing you notice is that the problems that brought you to therapy have disappeared.

　　1. What happened?

_____

_____

　　2. What changed?

_____

_____

Part II

For this second part, please refer back to the method you chose in Part I. Next, complete the questions in this section to further develop the vision of the future without the problem.

　　1. What happened to the problem?

_____

_____

2. How was the problem resolved?

_____

_____

3. What did you or others do?

_____

_____

4. What would it take to begin resolving your concern in the way you described?

_____

_____

II.13   I Can See Clearly Now: Developing a Future Focus

Therapist's Overview

Purpose of the Exercise

Processes aimed at helping people to change begin with well-articulated visions of the future. In this book, we offered specific ways of orienting clients to the futures they want for themselves. These futures represent clients' visions of what their lives will be like when their concerns have been resolved or minimized so they are manageable or less intrusive. This means working with clients to determine what they want to have happening in their future lives instead of the problems that have been interfering in the present.

Some techniques, despite being creative and clever, will not fit well with some clients and will not result in useful information. There are clients with whom the use of straightforward questions will provide a better alternative. Recall that therapeutic technique contributes very little to the overall variance in outcome. On the other hand, a future focus has been identified as crucial to successful therapy. Our task is to help orient clients toward their preferred futures without becoming overly reliant on any one method for achieving this. There are many possibilities, and the ones that are best will be the ones that fit with clients, are respectful, and are flexible. The purpose of this exercise is to offer an alternative to more technique-driven methods by providing questions to help clients articulate their visions of the future. We can help clients to work backward to outline steps and take action toward making those visions reality.

This exercise can be used at any point where focus is needed, particularly in determining what needs to change or be different for clients. It can be used at the start of services, in conjunction with establishing goals, or at any juncture when goals have been modified or changed altogether.

Suggestions for Use

1. Familiarize clients with "action-talk."
2. There are times when clients will create visions of the future that appear unattainable or unrealistic. It is important to acknowledge their viewpoints and work to further shape those visions to determine which aspects clients can work on in the present or immediate future. For example, if a client's vision were to have a parent back who passed away, the therapist might inquire as to what difference that would make for the client. From this the therapist learns that the client felt understood by her parent. The therapist could then help the client to explore her life for, or how to develop, other relationships in which she could feel understood more often than she is currently. The aim is to determine not only what clients want different in their futures, but what that difference symbolizes for them.
3. Although some clients will develop more elaborate visions, it is not necessary. Work to help clients develop a vision of some aspect of their future where things are going better. This could mean complete problem resolution or a reduction of the intensity or severity of concerns such that their lives are improved.
4. Cross-references: This activity can be used in combination with Exercise II.11, "Future Screening: Creating a Vision for the Future" and Exercise II.12, "Destination Imagination: Envisioning the Future Through Miracles, Dreams, and the Extraterrestrial." It also involves the use of "action-talk." To learn about this, please refer to the activity in Exercise II.7, "What Does That Look Like? Translating Ambiguity Through Action-Talk."

Exercise

This exercise is to help picture a time in the future in which things are going better and the problems you have been experiencing recently have gone away or are at least more manageable. From there you can identify ways of making that vision a reality. To complete this exercise, please answer the following questions by writing your responses in the spaces provided.

Find a time and a place when you can spend a few minutes by yourself and can clear your mind just a bit. You do not have to remove all that is going on in your head. You just want to be able to focus momentarily on thoughts other than your daily tasks and what needs to be done the remainder of the day.

Next, in whatever way works best for you, imagine yourself sometime in the future (a few weeks, months, or years) in a time when your current concerns and problems have lessened or gone away altogether. Try focusing on that vision and developing the details of it. As you do this, focus specifically on what is happening that you like—those parts of the image portray the kind of future you really want for yourself. When you are ready, answer the questions that follow.

Describe your vision and what is happening that really portrays the kind of future you want.

1. Be specific and use "action-talk" to describe what you are doing.

_____

_____

_____

_____

_____

2. How does the picture you described differ from the image you have of your life currently?

_____

_____

_____

_____

_____

3. What specifically contributed to things changing for the better?

_____

_____

_____

_____

4. What did you do? What did others do?

_____

_____

_____

_____

5. Try to break down the events that lead to things changing for the better. List a few of the steps that preceded your future vision.

    a. _____

    b. _____

    c. _____

    d. _____

    e. _____

6. Next, take one of the steps you outlined and break it into smaller steps.

    Step: _____

    Smaller Steps

    a. _____

    b. _____

    c. _____

7. What do you need to do to take one of the smaller steps?

_____

_____

_____

8. What challenges, if any, might you face in carrying out one or more of the steps you described?

_____

_____

9. What can you do to meet those challenges and take those initial steps?

_____

_____

Over the next day or two, put into action what you described in this exercise.

II.14   *From Here to Where? Service Planning for Change*

Therapist's Overview

Purpose of the Exercise

Most settings require some means of planning and writing out a course of action or service (treatment) plan for each client. This minimally translates to charting goals, outcomes, and means to these ends. Depending on the setting, funding stipulations, and other requirements, this can be an elaborate or simple process. The purpose of this exercise is to determine how to collaborate with clients to chart a course of action. It represents a map of what clients want to have different. This exercise can be used at the beginning of services or at any point at which it may be helpful to redefine the course of action. It is important to keep in mind that a client's particular path to change may be different than what is in written form. This exercise is meant to clarify and create direction, not to be deterministic.

To use this exercise, first complete Exercise II.8, "G-O! Focusing on Goals and Outcomes." Information from that exercise will be translated directly to this one.

Suggestions for Use

1. This exercise involves the use of "action-talk." To learn about this, please refer to the activity in Exercise II.7, "What Does That Look Like? Translating Ambiguity Through Action-Talk."
2. Take steps to ensure that what goes into service planning is representative of what clients want to have change. Service planning is a collaborative endeavor.
3. Make sure that what clients want included in service plans is realistic and attainable.
4. Identify small indicators of change.
5. Cross-references: This activity can be used in combination with Exercise II.13, "I Can See Clearly Now: Developing a Future Focus"; Exercise II.11, "Future Screening: Creating a Vision for the Future"; and Exercise II.12, "Destination Imagination: Envisioning the Future Through Miracles, Dreams, and the Extraterrestrial."

Exercise

This exercise is to clarify the plan for change. This is sometimes called a service or treatment plan. We prefer to think of it as an agreement about what needs to change. To complete this exercise, first refer to your responses from the exercise in exercise II.8, "G-O! Focusing on Goals and Outcomes." Next, please write your answers to the following questions in the spaces provided.

1. Collaborative service planning involves several key areas. The first is goals. In the blanks provided below, write down two or three of your goal descriptions.

Goal Description for #1

_____

_____

   Progress Indicator

_____

_____

Step

_____

Step

_____

Progress Indicator

_____

_____

Step

_____

Step

_____

Goal Description for #2

_____

_____

Progress Indicator

_____

_____

Step

_____

Step

_____

Progress Indicator

_____

_____

Step

_____

Step

_____

_____

Goal Description for #3

_____

_____

Progress Indicator

_____

_____

Step

_____

Step

_____

Progress Indicator

_____

_____

Step

_____

Step

_____

2. A second aspect of collaborative service planning is to determine progress toward established goals. Under each goal description, write down one or two small progress indicators that you are making to progress toward that goal. Be sure to make the indicators reasonable for you and use action-talk to ensure that they are clear.

3. Now it is time to move on to a third aspect. For each progress indicator, write down two concrete actions you can take to begin to work toward it. You can also write down things you may already be doing.

4. A fourth step is to transfer the outcome indicators from the "G-O!" exercise to the spaces below.

Outcome Indicators for Goal #1

    a. _____

    b. _____

Outcome Indicators for Goal #2

    a. _____

    b. _____

Outcome Indicators for Goal #3

    a. _____

    b. _____

5. Last, describe how your situation or life will be different as a result of achieving improvement with one or more outcomes.

_____

_____

_____

_____

All that is left now is to follow the plan!

II.15   *In Many Ways: Mapping Paths of Change*

Therapist's Overview

Purpose of the Exercise

As we learned through other exercises, expectations often lead the way in therapy. Clients not only have ideas about how they expect therapy to take place, they also have expectations about how they expect change to take place. The purpose of this exercise is to explore clients' ideas and expectations for change. This exercise will help us to better understand how change has occurred in the past with clients and how they expect it to occur with their current concerns. Therapists can then incorporate those ideas into therapy and increase the prospects of positive outcome by using methods that provide a great degree of fit for clients.

Suggestions for Use

1. This exercise can be used with individuals, couples, and families. Be reminded that with couples and families, there are likely to be different perspectives represented. It may therefore be useful to have each person complete his or her own worksheet and then seek to identify common themes that illustrate clients' overall expectations.
2. Because clients' expectations can change over time, it is important to maintain ongoing conversations to monitor for those changes and incorporate new or modified expectations into therapy.
3. Cross-references: This exercise can be used in conjunction with Exercise I.8, "The Key Is Collaboration: Working "With" Clients" and Exercise I.9, "Expectations and Next-Pectations: Learning Clients' Preferences for Therapy."

Exercise

We all experience change in our lives. When we take the time to explore how various changes occurred, we often learn about specific factors that contributed to those changes. One of these is the expectations we have. In therapy, our ideas around how we expect change to occur are important to change. The more your therapist knows about how you expect change to occur, the more he or she can work with you in ways that you see as most beneficial. Therefore, this exercise is to help you and your therapist to better understand your expectations for change. To complete this exercise, please answer the questions below and write your responses in the spaces provided.

1. How do things usually change in your life?

_____

_____

2. What usually prompts or initiates change for you?

_____

_____

3. How do you usually go about trying to resolve your concerns or problems?

_____

_____

_____

4. What have you done in the past to resolve your concerns or problems?

_____

_____

_____

5. What ideas do you have about how change is going to take place with your concern, problem, or situation?

_____

_____

_____

6. What ideas have you considered that might assist with your concern, problem, or situation?

_____

_____

_____

7. If you had this idea about someone else, what would you suggest he or she do to resolve it?

_____

_____

_____

8. What has to happen before the change you are seeking occurs?

_____

_____

_____

9. At what rate (for example, slow or fast) do you expect change to occur?

_____

_____

_____

10. Will change likely be in big amounts, small amounts, or incremental?

_____

_____

_____

11. Do you expect change to occur by viewing things differently? By doing something different? By others doing something different?

_____

_____

_____

II.16   *The Spokes of Life: Cultivating Resources*

Therapist's Overview

Purpose of the Exercise

Clients have resources within their relationships and social systems. These systems of support are essential to building solutions and promoting change. This exercise is designed to help in the identification of social supports in the form of relationships and other external systems that can be used to build connections, increase stability, and facilitate positive change.

Suggestions for Use

1. This exercise can be completed as part of initial information-gathering (assessment) processes or as a stand-alone activity in or outside of therapy.
2. It is not necessary for clients to fill in something for each area. There are many possible combinations. Clients may have many resources in one area, a consistent distribution, a smattering in different areas, and so on. The important thing is to help clients to expand their immediate system to include past, present, and potential future resources that can be helpful with current concerns.

Exercise

When faced with challenges, it can be easy to overlook the past, present, and potential future contributions of others. This could be in the form of family, friends, colleagues at work or school, and so on. Associations with such persons may be consistent, occasional, ongoing, or random. The key is to identify people, groups, or systems that may be of support with the problem(s) you are currently facing. To complete this exercise, please complete Part I by first identifying these persons or entities. Consider how they might be a resource to you or in your relationships. At this point, it is not important to know whether or not a potential form of support will actually pan out. We only want to think as creatively as possible, casting a wide net in identifying resources we might not have initially noticed or considered as helpful to us. In Part II please consider how you can begin to further explore the resources you identified.

Part I

Please list and describe past, present, or potential future resources for you and your family or relationship.

1. Client Name_____

   Qualities/Characteristics _____

   Abilities/Strengths _____

   Hobbies/Interests_____

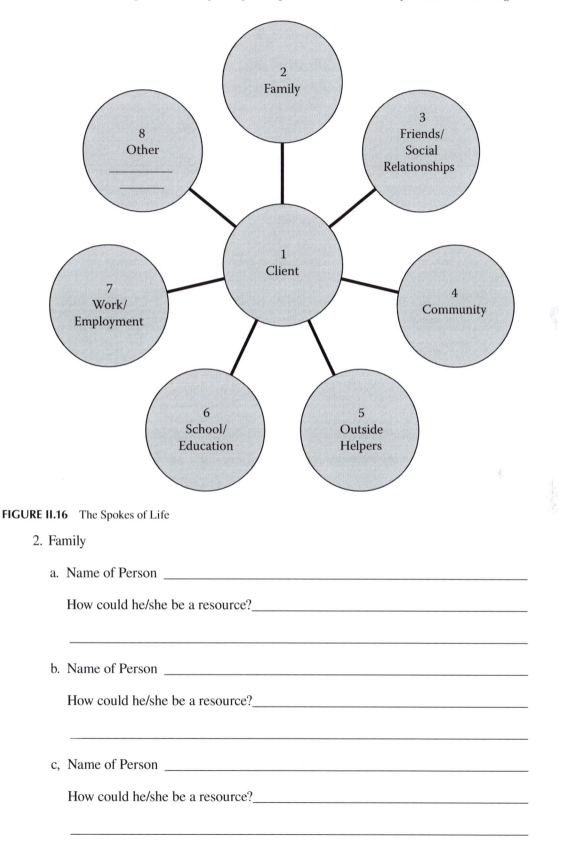

FIGURE II.16   The Spokes of Life

2. Family

   a. Name of Person _____

      How could he/she be a resource?_____

      _____

   b. Name of Person _____

      How could he/she be a resource?_____

      _____

   c, Name of Person _____

      How could he/she be a resource?_____

      _____

3. Friends/Social Relationships

    a. Name of Person_____

       How could he/she be a resource? _____

       _____

    b. Name of Person_____

       How could he/she be a resource? _____

       _____

    c. Name of Person_____

       How could he/she be a resource? _____

       _____

4. Community

    a. Type of Resource_____

       Name of Person_____

       How could he/she be a resource? _____

       _____

    b. Type of Resource _____

       Name of Person_____

       How could he/she be a resource? _____

       _____

5. Outside Helpers (i.e., counselor, social worker, case manager, probation/juvenile offi-
   cer, or other)

    a. Name of Person_____

       How could he/she be a resource? _____

    b. Name of Person_____

       How could he/she be a resource? _____

6. School/Education

   a Name of Person _____

      How could he/she be a resource? _____

   b. Name of Person_____

      How could he/she be a resource? _____

   c. Name of Person_____

      How could he/she be a resource? _____

   d. Name of Person_____

      How could he/she be a resource?_____

7. Work/Employment

   a. Name of Person _____

      How could he/she be a resource? _____

   b. Name of Person_____

      How could he/she be a resource? _____

   c. Name of Person_____

      How could he/she be a resource? _____

   d. Name of Person_____

      How could he/she be a resource?_____

8. Other (please name)

   a. Name of Person _____

      How could he/she be a resource? _____

   b. Name of Person_____

      How could he/she be a resource? _____

   c. Name of Person_____

      How could he/she be a resource? _____

d. Name of Person_____

    How could he/she be a resource?_____

Part II

Please complete the following questions.

    1. What would be a first step in further exploring these resources?

_____

_____

_____

_____

    2. What can you do to make this happen a little bit now?

_____

_____

_____

_____

II.17   *What Tips the Scale? Weighing the Benefits of Change*

Therapist's Overview

Purpose of the Exercise

Therapy that maximizes the capacities for change is properly matched with clients' levels of motivation and their state of readiness to change. One way of learning about client motivation is by engaging in conversations aimed at determining the possible benefits of positive change or "changing for the good." This process can help clients to convince themselves that the benefits of taking actions to achieve positive change outweigh the drawbacks of remaining "as is" and taking no action. The purpose of this exercise is to help clients weigh the "pros and cons" and, in effect, tip the scale such that taking action in new, more beneficial ways is the preferred course.

Suggestions for Use

1. This exercise can be used at different points in therapy and whenever it appears helpful to assist clients with weighing the benefits of positive change.
2. This exercise can be completed with clients or can be given to them to complete on their own. It can also be used to generate questions in therapy.
3. This exercise can be used in its entirety or in parts. Due to its length, for some clients it can be helpful to have people complete it in sequences or to use fewer questions.

Exercise

Although change is a constant in people's lives, it is not always clear what state of readiness they are in to act on their concerns. There are times when people will appear ambivalent or less open to making plans and taking action. We do not see people as unmotivated but instead motivated for some things and less for others. This exercise can assist with helping people to weigh the pros and cons of making changes or letting their situations remain "as is." The idea is that through activities such as this, people will convince themselves that there is greater benefit in taking action. To complete this exercise, please have your client answer the questions below. Write the answers in the spaces provided. Due to the number of questions in this exercise, you may want to split it up over a couple of sittings.

Disadvantages of the Status Quo

1. What concerns or worries you about your current situation? How has that affected you?

_____

_____

_____

2. What kinds of hardships has your current situation contributed to?

_____

_____

_____

3. In what ways does that concern you?

_____

_____

_____

4. How might it be a concern for you if you decided to leave your situation alone?

_____

_____

_____

5. What do you think will happen if you decide to not change anything with your situation?

_____

_____

_____

Advantages/Benefits of Change

1. How would you like things to be different?

_____

_____

_____

2. What might it be like for you with your situation improved?

_____

_____

_____

3. Looking a few days/weeks/months/years into the future to a time when things are improved with your current situation, what might your life be like?

_____

_____

_____

4. What would be some of the advantages or benefits of things changing with your current situation?

_____

_____

_____

5. What would be advantages or benefits in you taking action to make changes?

_____

_____

_____

6. How might others benefit from changes you made?

_____

_____

_____

Optimism About Change

1. What affects your sense of optimism that you can make changes with your current situation?

_____

_____

_____

2. What makes you think that you can make the changes you want, should you decide to?

_____

_____

_____

3. What encourages you or gives you hope that you can achieve the change you want?

_____

_____

_____

4. How confident are you that you can make changes with your situation?

_____

_____

_____

5. What experience in making changes can you draw on that might be helpful to you with your current situation?

_____

_____

_____

6. What strengths might be helpful to you in making this change?

_____

_____

_____

7. What external resources (people, relationships, support systems) might be helpful to you in making this change?

_____

_____

_____

Intention to Change

1. What is your stance on your concern?

_____

_____

_____

2. What are your thoughts about it?

_____

_____

_____

3. What are your intentions?

_____

_____

_____

4. How important is it to you for things to change with your current situation?

_____

_____

_____

5. What kinds of factors are currently influencing what you might do?

_____

_____

_____

6. What might you be willing to try?

_____

_____

_____

7. Of the possibilities discussed so far, which one(s) are most appealing to you?

_____

_____

_____

8. What would it take for you to begin to take a step toward changing your situation?

_____

_____

_____

After completing these questions take some time to reflect on your answers, and if you are seeing a therapist, consider talking with him or her about your current position on your concern(s) or situations.

II.18   Embracing Your State: A Race With Yourself

Therapist's Overview

Purpose of the Exercise

When examining personality development theories, one will find similarities in the definitions of what constitutes being psychologically healthy. In general, a person is psychologically healthy when he or she can determine and live by values and beliefs that are internal to them while at the same time not having those values and beliefs harm others. A major step in maintaining a healthy psychological self is being able to separate external societal ideas of normalcy that do not match personal values. The more individuals can gauge their development against personal markers and less against societal markers, the more psychologically healthy they will become.

The intent of this exercise is to expand this idea of identifying clients' ideas of healthy functioning to create their new normal. How can clients identify ways in which their normal is similar and different from societal values to produce continued healthy psychological development? Perhaps the essential starting point for clients is their recognition and acceptance of where they are in their life. All individuals have ideas of "where they should be" and have to personally determine how well they are meeting their goals. The ability for the counselor to match their client's stage of change is an essential task for the success of this exercise. When the counselor and the client are in congruence regarding the counseling process, the client will be better able to internalize change and relearn their values and beliefs.

Suggestions for Use

1. This exercise can be beneficial early in the counseling process as a means to identify goals.
2. This exercise can be helpful when new concerns arise to help determine the client's stage of change and ways to match their readiness for change.
3. Another situation in which to utilize this exercise is when you are discussing the possibility of ending counseling. The exercise can gauge, from the client's perspective, how psychologically healthy the client is and areas for further examination.

Exercise

To begin this exercise, ask your client the following questions.

1. What aspects of your life are important to you?

_____

_____

2. How did you develop those important aspects of your life?

_____

_____

3. How can you continue to develop important areas of your life?

_____

_____

4. When you have accomplished something, how do you know you did a good job?

_____

_____

5. What indicators do you utilize that help you gauge your progress?

_____

_____

6. What aspects of yourself help you make and sustain change?

_____

_____

7. Examining your current complaint, what are you ready to do to get just a little more understanding of it?

_____

_____

8. What signs in your life will you be able to recognize that will indicate you have your complaint under control?

_____

_____

9. How will you know when you feel normal in your own skin?

_____

_____

II.19   Matching Up: Creating a Fit Between Therapist and Client

Therapist's Overview

Purpose of the Exercise

One of the ways that we can increase the chances of clients benefiting from therapy and achieving positive outcomes is by improving the match between clients' ideas and therapists' approaches. An SSB approach is reliant on therapists incorporating clients' perceptions, preferences, coping styles, and so on, as a means of selecting methods. The purpose of this exercise is to elicit client information as a means of determining which techniques increase the "factor of fit."

Suggestions for Use

1. This exercise can be used at different points in therapy but is most applicable at the beginning of therapy.
2. This exercise can be completed with clients or can be given to them to complete on their own. It can also be used to generate questions in therapy.
3. This exercise works well as part of those exercises listed under Cross-references.
4. Cross-references: See Exercise I.8, "The Key Is Collaboration: Working 'With' Clients"; Exercise I.9, "Expectations and Next-Pectations: Learning Clients' Preferences for Therapy"; Exercise II.15, "In Many Ways: Mapping Paths of Change"; and Exercise II.17, "What Tips the Scale? Weighing the Benefits of Change."

Exercise

Successful therapy hinges on the match between clients' ideas and preferences and therapists' approaches. A good fit increases the likelihood of change, whereas a lack of good fit can lead to premature dropout and poorer outcomes. This exercise is to help you gather further information from clients as a means of selecting methods that meet clients' needs and are respectful of their ideas about change. To complete this exercise, please write your responses in the spaces provided.

1. How does the client describe his/her/their concerns or problems (for example, experientially, cognitively, in action or interactional terms, or in some combination)?

_____

_____

_____

_____

2. What are clients' ideas about change (in other words, how and under what conditions do they expect change to occur)?

_____

_____

_____

_____

3. What cultural influences might affect their perceptions about change?

_____

_____

_____

_____

4. How do clients describe their relationships with concerns or problems (in other words, how involved do they see themselves with the concerns raised)?

_____

_____

_____

_____

5. What is the client's primary coping style? (Internal/External)

_____

_____

_____

_____

6. In general, at what stage of change does the client appear to be?

_____

_____

_____

_____

Use this information along with that gathered from other exercises to select methods and techniques that fit with clients and increase the prospects of positive change.

II.20   The Filing Cabinet: Categorizing My Favorite Methods

Therapist's Overview

Purpose of the Exercise

We all have our favorite methods and techniques. And yet we have learned that method accounts for little of the overall variance in therapeutic outcomes. When selecting and using methods, we want to consider how they fit with clients' expectations of change and how they tap into the foundational principles of SSB therapies. The purpose of this exercise is to identify favorite methods and file or categorize them under the overarching realms of change that therapy models work within. This can provide a template for selecting and matching methods as therapy progresses, thereby increasing the factor of fit between the client's expectations for change and the therapist's approach.

Suggestions for Use

1. This exercise is for therapists or for any professional or student who works in the helping professions.
2. Because practitioners tend to add to their "filing cabinets" as they learn more and gain experience, it is a good idea to revisit this activity periodically to update the files.
3. Cross-reference: This exercise can be used in conjunction with each of the exercises listed in Sections IV through VI.

Exercise

As therapists, we are exposed to numerous methods and techniques. Some of these stick with us, and others do not. The issue with methods is twofold: (a) whether they fit with and complement clients' ideas, expectations, and orientations to change; and (b) how they tap into and activate the foundational principles of SSB therapies. This exercise will help you to identify and "file" your favorite methods, thereby having them at your fingertips and available if needed in a given situation. To complete this exercise, please follow the directions below.

In the spaces provided below, make a list of the methods and techniques you used and found helpful. This can also include favorites that you use infrequently but place value in.

_____   _____

_____   _____

_____   _____

_____   _____

_____   _____

_____   _____

Next, take a moment to familiarize yourself with the primary realms of change associated with SSB. These include *Experience, Perceptions and Perspectives,* and *Action and Interaction.* Each of these areas focuses on helping clients to change one or more aspect of their lives and functioning and is described in detail in the introduction to this book. *Experience* involves emotion, affect, feelings, sensory experience, and sense of self. *Perceptions and Perspectives* relate to client beliefs, assumptions, views, stories, and patterns of attention. *Action and Interaction* have to do with clients' behaviors, individual actions, and ways of relating.

To complete this section, please revisit the methods you listed earlier in this exercise and place them under the category that provides the best "umbrella" for that method. If a particular method crosses over into two or more categories, please list it separately under each.

Experience	Perceptions and Perspectives	Action and Interaction

Keep this file of your methods handy in the event that you are searching for an idea for a particular situation. It is also a good practice to revisit this file periodically so it can be kept up to date.w

II.21   Song for Myself: Celebrating Strength, Capacity, and Individuality

Therapist's Overview

Purpose of the Exercise

At times, clients are encountered who have difficulty identifying their own strengths and capacities. For these individuals, circumstances may be such that they are continually given internal and external messages that inhibit their ability to galvanize that in their lives that may be brought to the assistance of their concerns. A structured activity can sometimes be helpful in fostering a new perspective on the self and the environment. Once strengths are more overtly identified, the client will have a firmer understanding of their own ability to effect change.

This exercise is beneficial for use at the beginning of services. It can be helpful to use while establishing goals and creating a future focus.

Suggestions for Use

1. Children and adolescents may find this exercise and homework helpful in thinking about individual traits and strengths in a way that may be developmentally challenging for them.
2. Very young clients may have the homework completed by an adult who is in a position to know them well and observe them frequently.

Exercise

Initial Questions

1. Who is someone, either in your life or whom you have seen on television or in movies, who seems happy and successful to you?

_____

_____

2. What do you think makes him or her happy and successful?

_____

_____

3. What qualities does he or she possess that contributes to his or her happiness?

   a. _____

   b. _____

   c. _____

   d. _____

   e. _____

   f. _____

4. What do each of these qualities look like to you?

a. _____

b. _____

c. _____

d. _____

e. _____

f. _____

Task

Over the next week, I would like you to write down the times when you displayed these traits or qualities.

Trait A _____

Situation 1

_____

_____

Situation 2

_____

_____

How did you feel when you displayed this trait or quality?

_____

_____

Trait B _____

Situation 1

_____

_____

Situation 2

_____

_____

How did you feel when you displayed this trait or quality?

_____

_____

Trait C _____

Situation 1

_____

_____

Situation 2

_____

_____

How did you feel when you displayed this trait or quality?

_____

_____

Trait D _____

Situation 1

_____

_____

Situation 2

_____

_____

How did you feel when you displayed this trait or quality?

_____

_____

Trait E _____

   Situation 1

_____

_____

   Situation 2

_____

_____

   How did you feel when you displayed this trait or quality?

_____

_____

Trait F _____

   Situation 1

_____

_____

   Situation 2

_____

_____

   How did you feel when you displayed this trait or quality?

_____

_____

Please bring this worksheet with you for your next session.

SECTION III

RECONNECTION TO SELF
Experience, Affect, and Emotion

III.1   *Getting in Touch With Emotion: Hearing What Feelings Have to Say*

Therapist's Overview

Purpose of the Exercise

Traditionally, emotional states are often used minimally or overlooked entirely with other strengths and solution-based (SSB) techniques. However, it can often be the case that while collaborating with your clients, identifying and emphasizing both their own and your own particular emotional states can be powerful tools to enhance change. The purpose of this exercise, then, is to operate as a guide toward utilizing emotion as a therapeutic device.

Often an initial attempt at being personally congruent and empathizing with the client can create an atmosphere where emotion can be more fully explored. Simply "being" with a client while they are experiencing various emotions during counseling is as effective as any exercise. As is generally acknowledged, basic nonverbal communication techniques usually demonstrate your own comfortableness with emotion and thence model the behavior for your client. This type of work with emotional states and awareness is representative of the exercise below.

Suggestions for Use

1. This exercise may be beneficial for any professional who would like to capitalize more on emotion while counseling.
2. This exercise can be helpful for any individual who is developmentally aware of their emotions and how they impact their life.
3. Before starting any session, take a few minutes to get in tune with your emotional state so you will be ready to communicate effectively with your client. A relaxed counselor has a better chance to be an effective counselor. Moreover, if you are unsure whether or not to focus on emotion, be sure to ask your client his or her preference.
4. Cross-references: This exercise can be effectively used with exercises in Section I when examining counseling style and worldview.

Exercise

Here are a few questions to ask yourself and your client to better utilize emotions while counseling.

1. In what ways are you aware of your emotional preferences?

_____

_____

2. When you are experiencing a time of difficulty, how do you prefer significant others in your life to interact with you?

_____

_____

3. How can you increase the preferred way that these significant individuals interact with you to coincide with your emotional preferences?

_____

_____

4. What word(s) would you use to describe your ideal emotional state?

_____

_____

5. How would you describe your "everyday" emotional state?

_____

_____

6. Describe one way you could benefit from knowing your emotional preferences.

_____

_____

III.2   The Culture of Emotion: Aligning Emotion and Change

Therapist's Overview

Purpose of the Exercise

Emotions, as with most behaviors and norms, are highly cultural. All individuals have individual, familial, and larger communal influences on emotional development and expression. Recognizing and collaborating with your clients on how their culture views emotion may be beneficial in the change process. Moreover, it would make sense that misidentifying cultural norms regarding emotion may decrease the therapeutic relationship. The purpose of this exercise is to become better informed regarding your clients' preferred emotional norms.

Suggestions for Use

1. This exercise may be beneficial for any professional who would like to capitalize more on emotion while counseling.
2. This exercise can be helpful for any individual who is developmentally aware of their emotions and how they impact our life.
3. This exercise can be effectively used with Exercise III.1, "Getting in Touch With Emotion: Hearing What Feelings Have to Say."

Exercise

To begin this exercise, take note of your client and ask yourself these questions.

1. What outward or verbal emotional indicators (if any) does your client express (do they seem sad, happy, etc.)?
2. In the context of counseling, has your client stated that he or she or significant others are highly emotional (or are not emotional)?
3. Has your client stated that "In my family, we just do not talk about emotion." Or has your client identified times when he or she expresses or does not express emotion (e.g., a parent not crying in front of children).

Paying attention to cues given to you during the normal process of counseling may help to better utilize emotion to strengthen change and not decrease the therapeutic alliance. Similar questions can be asked to your clients for them to capitalize on emotion in their life. The following are a few questions to ask.

1. What role does emotion play in your and your family's life?

_____

_____

2. In what ways can emotion make your life just a little bit better?

_____

_____

3. Have there been times when emotion helped or hindered your daily activities?

_____

_____

4. Describe the context in which emotion helped or hindered your daily activities.

_____

_____

5. How can you take that knowledge and use it to your advantage?

_____

_____

III.3   *Flipping the Switch: Tuning In To Self*

Therapist's Overview

Purpose of the Exercise

People have preferred ways of orienting to the world around them. Some people tend to be more cognitive, intellectualizing events, experiences, and their lives. Others, whether daily, weekly, or otherwise, engage in activities that involve changing the way they act or interact with others. Still others focus on feeling states including their emotions and feelings. People can also move between different ways of orienting to the world, switching from thinking to action, for example. For people who tend to neglect their emotions and feelings, it can be helpful to suggest a shift to focusing more on their internal states. The benefits can be an increased relaxation, calmness, and improved sense of well-being. The purpose of this exercise is to invite people into ways of increasing greater degrees of experiential connections to self.

Suggestions for Use

1. This exercise can be used at any point in therapy.
2. It is not necessary for people to focus on or remain in the experiential or emotional domain for long periods of time. The aim is to invite them to reconnect with themselves as well as recognize the value of emotions.
3. We want to invite, not coerce or push people in directions that they are not interested in moving in. If a particular client is not interested in or declines an invitation to focus on internal experience, it is important to respect this preference.

Exercise

It is likely that you have a preferred way of approaching life. You may be more of a thinker or more of a doer. Or you may prefer to focus more on your interactions with others. One particular way to address concerns is to tune into your feelings or emotions and become more aware of your emotional states. If this is new for you or perhaps a little uncomfortable, that is understandable as sometimes immersing oneself in emotion can bring out feelings that have been kept at bay.

If this is not your preferred way of orienting to the world, perhaps you might consider how tuning into yourself creates a new experience for you. It is not necessary to do this on a regular basis, and if now is not the time for you, you can always revisit this exercise in the future.

To complete this exercise, please follow the instructions listed below. Next, write your responses in the spaces provided.

1. First, on a scale of 1 to 10, in which 1 represents "very tense" and 10 represents "not tense at all," what number would you rate yourself at right now? _____

2. Find a place that is relatively quiet and free of distractions. You will need about 10 minutes for this exercise. If possible, review the sequence that follows so you can run through the different parts in your mind without having to continue to refer back to the steps in written form.

    a. Sit in a chair or on the floor and allow your body to relax.
    b. Take three deep breaths. Slowly inhale through the nose and exhale through the mouth. You may choose to close your eyes.

    c. Let your mind wander for a moment or two. Whatever enters your mind is perfectly fine. Just let it be there.

    d. Begin to notice any emotions, feelings, or bodily sensations you may have. Just let them exist, knowing that you are safe.

    e. When you are ready, take another three deep breaths, the same as you did earlier. If you closed your eyes, slowly open them and reorient to the current place, time, and context.

3. Now, please answer the following questions associated with your experience.

    a. On a scale of 1 to 10, with 1 representing "not at all" and 10 representing "fully immersed," what level (number) did you get to in your brief experience? _____

    b. How was the overall experience for you? What did you notice about it?

_____

_____

_____

_____

    c. What kinds of emotions, feelings, and bodily sensations did you notice? What was that like for you?

_____

_____

_____

_____

    d. What was the result of tuning into yourself? What, if anything, did you learn about yourself?

_____

_____

_____

_____

4. Finally, on a scale of 1 to 10, in which 1 represents "very tense" and 10 represents "not tense at all," what number would you rate yourself at right now? _____

Hopefully you found this to be a positive experience and one that you can do for short or long periods of time. By tuning into your emotions, feelings, and bodily sensations, you can become more aware of how you experience the world and the connections between thoughts and feelings. This can lead to more internal calmness, relaxation, and awareness about relationships to self, others, and the world around you.

III.4   *"And" Now for Something Completely Different: The Use of Words to Build New Connections*

Therapist's Overview

Purpose of the Exercise

Whether through our own thoughts or the voices of society, there are many ways that our experiences, thoughts, and perceptions can seem contradictory, contributing to increased levels of stress. This commonly occurs when two or more experiences or ideas appear to stand in opposition to one another. Examples might include, "If I don't get my medicine I can't control myself," "I could get my work done but not with her nagging me," or "I can't have any anxiety when I take tests." In some instances, such contradictions or injunctions are created by experiencing two or more things that appear in conflict of one another. The purpose of this exercise is to work toward reconciling these contradictions through the use of the word "and" instead of the word "but" (whether stated directly or implied). This allows for both experiences to exist simultaneously.

Suggestions for Use

1. This exercise can be used at any point in therapy.
2. Beyond a stand-alone method, the use of the word "and" is a good practice in general for therapists who are working toward helping clients create room within their experience for what can appear to be contradictory experiences.

Exercise

There are times when the experiences and perceptions we have appear to be in conflict with one another. The word "but" is either directly present or implied in our thoughts or statements. For example, we might think or say, "I could be a much better parent but I'm so busy with work" or "If I don't get enough sleep, then people can expect that I will be less tolerant." These injunctions reflect what appear to be contradictory experiences or thoughts. They are often the result of not allowing enough room within ourselves for two seemingly different aspects. This exercise is to help to create more room within your experience by changing your language through the use of the word "and." To complete this exercise, please write your responses in the spaces provided.

Consider the following statements:

- I would be able to control my anger if people would just leave me alone.
- I can't stop eating when people keep putting food in front of me.
- I'd be happy but not if my work situation stays the same.
- I'm not a good student if I get anything other than an "A."

What did you notice about the above statements?

_____

_____

The dilemma with such statements is that they imply that one component of experience is not possible with the presence of another. In other words, these statements either directly or indirectly imply that one cannot change without the other changing. Not only can these statements close down possibilities for change, they can diminish accountability.

One response to these statements is to connect what appear to be contradictory experiences and perceptions either directly or indirectly through the word "and." Consider the previous examples, and we will see how this works.

Original Statement:
- I would be able to control my anger if people would just leave me alone.

Alternative Statements:
- I can control my anger even when people don't leave me alone.
- I can be angry and respond respectfully despite what others do.

Original Statement:
- I can't stop eating when people keep putting food in front of me.

Alternative Statements:
- I can be in control of my eating and accept that sometimes there will be food in front of me that is hard to resist.
- I can stop eating too much even when I am in situations where there is a lot of food.

Original Statement:
- I could be happy but not if my work situation stays the same.

Alternative Statements:
- I can be happy despite my work situation.
- I can be happy and my work situation can stay the same.

Original Statement:
- I'm not a good student if I get anything other than an "A."

Alternative Statements:
- I can be a good student even if I don't get an "A" in every assignment and class.
- I can be a good student and not have to get an "A" on everything.

What are the statements with injunctions you find yourself making? Write down two to three of these.

1. _____

2. _____

3. _____

Next, write how you can change these statements through use of the word "and."

1. _____

2. _____

3. _____

In the future, consider how you can use the word "and" to create room within yourself for what can appear to be contradictory experiences or thoughts.

III.5   In a Moment's Notice: Internalizing the Experience of Now

Therapist's Overview

Purpose of the Exercise

Just as people can shift between ways of orienting to the world (i.e., experience/emotion, views/ cognitions, actions/interactions), it is common to focus attention primarily on the past, present, or future. Although each of these domains can serve people well, depending on the circumstances, it is also possible that too narrow a focus can inhibit progress. In other words, being too much in the past, present, or future, at the expense of the other aspects can contribute to closed-down views in which people cannot see other possibilities that a focus on alternative domains can bring. The purpose of this exercise is to invite people who tend to focus too much on the past or the future to tune into the present to consider what possibilities might arise as a result.

Suggestions for Use

1. This exercise can be used at any point in therapy.
2. It is not necessary for people to remain present-focused for extended periods of time. The aim is to invite them to consider other possibilities that might result from shifting to a focus on the present.
3. We want to invite, not coerce or push people in directions that they are not interested in moving in. If a particular client is not interested in or declines an invitation to focus on the present, it is important to respect this preference.
4. This activity can be used to help people to shift to more of a past or future focus in the event that a person exists too much in the present. The idea is to help people move between different ways of relating to the world which, in turn, can bring about new possibilities.
5. Cross-reference: See Exercise III.3, "Flipping the Switch: Tuning In To Self."

Exercise

Although we all have general orientations that lead us to focus more predominantly on the past, present, or future, there are times when it can be helpful to shift toward a different domain. This exercise is to help you orient your attention to the present as a means of exploring new possibilities with the current concern(s) you are facing. The present may or may not be a focus you emphasized; however, noticing what is happening now can open up new pathways. To complete this exercise, please write your responses in the spaces provided.

1. Take a moment to reflect on the problem you are currently facing. Allow yourself to think about how it affects you in the present. Write down your thoughts and feelings below.

_____

_____

_____

_____

2. What do you notice about focusing on the problem in the present versus the past or future?

_____

_____

_____

_____

3. What are you more aware of now that perhaps was less evident to you previously?

_____

_____

_____

_____

4. What might you do as a result of this awareness?

_____

_____

_____

_____

5. How could you get that to happen a little bit now?

_____

_____

_____

_____

III.6   The 360° Self: Integrating Internal Experience and Aspects of Self

Therapist's Overview

Purpose of the Exercise

Carl Jung often spoke of the "shadow," those aspects or parts of our experience that represent the darker sides of ourselves. For most persons, life involves an ongoing process of accepting these sometimes intense and undesirable aspects of self, even though those aspects can sometimes produce discomfort. When people are able to accept and integrate all feelings, emotions, and sensations, they can achieve higher levels of balance and, more often, less symptoms that have been the result of disowned aspects of self. The purpose of this exercise is to invite people into ways of acknowledging, accepting, and integrating various aspects of self that were cast away or perhaps contributing to further pain and suffering. When all aspects are integrated, it can be said that a person has achieved a 360° self.

Suggestions for Use

1. This exercise can be used at any point in therapy.
2. It is sometimes difficult for people to integrate aspects of self that they labeled as negative. It is important that people are first invited to acknowledge what may have been cast away. Then, at their own rate and pace, people can move toward accepting and integrating those aspects.
3. We want to invite, not coerce or push people in directions that they are not interested in moving in. If a particular client is not interested in or declines an invitation to focus on disowned aspects, we want to be respectful of that.
4. Cross-reference: This exercise can be used with Exercise III.3, "Flipping the Switch: Tuning In To Self."

Exercise

Every person has an aspect of himself or herself that he or she would rather cast away and be rid of. Sometimes these aspects can surface in ways that are undesirable. For example, a person might say, "I never get angry." Anger might be seen as a bad or useless emotion. If that same person, however, is not accepting of anger, it is possible that anger will show up in some way in his or her life in an intrusive way. For example, the person might feel that he or she has been treated unjustly and instead of responding in a direct yet responsible way, he or she may fly into a rage; a response that is disproportionate to the situation. In other words, those aspects of self that are cast away are likely to show up in some way that causes further distress. This exercise is to identify internal experiences, particularly feelings and emotions, and begin to allow them to exist with ourselves. When we integrate these aspects, we develop a more balanced sense of self—one in which all aspects are acknowledged, accepted, and integrated. We refer to this as the 360° self.

To complete this exercise, please follow the instructions listed below. Next, write your responses in the spaces provided.

1. Think about the feelings and emotions you experience most often in your everyday life. List those feelings below:

_____ _____   _____ _____

_____ _____   _____ _____

_____ _____   _____ _____

_____ _____   _____ _____

_____ _____   _____ _____

_____ _____   _____ _____

2. Next, return to your list and on a scale of 1 to 10, in which 1 represents "not at all" and 10 represents "completely," rate how accepting you are of each feeling for yourself.

3. In the spaces below, write the feelings or emotions to which you assigned a rating of 3 or less.

_____ _____   _____ _____

_____ _____   _____ _____

_____ _____   _____ _____

4. Select one feeling or emotion you listed in Question #3 and then follow the process outlined beginning in Question #5.

    Feeling/Emotion: _____

5. Describe how a lower level of acceptance of this feeling or emotion contributed to your distress.

_____

_____

_____

_____

6. What, in your mind, do you see as a possible hurdle(s) to being more accepting of that feeling or emotion?

_____

_____

_____

_____

7. Picture your feeling or emotion as being a valuable part of you. The experience, whether good or bad, is part of you and does not have to dominate you. It can just be present as part of you. We call this *acknowledging* the aspect. In the spaces provided, write your thoughts about what it might be like for you to acknowledge that feeling or emotion. You do not have to do anything more than acknowledge what you feel.

_____

_____

_____

_____

8. When you are ready, consider steps you could need to take to begin to move from acknowledgment of the feeling or emotion to acceptance of it. In the spaces below, list up to three steps you might take.

a. _____

b. _____

c. _____

9. What will it take for you to begin to take the step(s) outlined in Question #8?

_____

_____

_____

_____

10. When you accept your feeling or emotion as real, legitimate, and as having some value, it is time to move on to the final part of the process.

11. Consider that every feeling and emotion you experience is part of you. We refer to this as *integration*. Integrating aspects of self does not necessarily mean we value all aspects similarly. It only means that we acknowledge an aspect, accept it, and allow it to exist as part of who we

are. We do not always like these parts of ourselves, particularly the darker ones, but we recognize they are part of us.

With this in mind, in the spaces below, answer the following question: "How do I allow _____ (Feeling/Emotion) to be part of me in a way that is not just acceptable to me but also part of who I am?

_____

_____

_____

_____

When you are done, give yourself some time and space to allow what you are working to integrate to exist without conflict. Integrating different aspects of self can be a process. If you get stuck, go back to the first part—acknowledge an aspect before trying to accept or integrate it. You can also repeat this process with the other aspects you listed in Question #3.

III.7 *Body Over Mind: Settling Down Through Abilities*

Therapist's Overview

Purpose of the Exercise

Research has indicated that some people, depending on their experiences, the situation, and other factors, will struggle when it comes to talking and, oftentimes, in being able to gather their thoughts and think clearly. This is because they will become "overloaded" from increased physiological activity in the region of the brain containing the amygdala and hypothalamus. In addition, the frontal cortex, which affects language, speech, and thinking, becomes inhibited. This can occur with people who experienced emotionally overwhelming events such as trauma, anxiety, or fear-producing events. In such cases, the body in effect overruns the mind. One way to help people through this is to use processes that help people to relax physiologically which ultimately frees them up to think more clearly and speak. The purpose of this exercise is to explore a way of helping clients to achieve calmness in their bodies such that they can engage in conversation without being physiologically overwhelmed.

Suggestions for Use

1. This exercise can be used at any point in therapy.
2. This exercise should be done with clients; however, a client can try it with another person with whom he or she feels safe. It can also be attempted without the aid of another person, although it is likely to be particularly challenging.
3. It can be helpful to notice key indicators that people are possibly being overwhelmed physiologically. These can include shaking, stuttering or stammering, difficulty speaking, quivering in the voice, broken speech, intense sweating, disconnected thoughts, and dissociation.
4. Therapists should always use their observing, listening, and attending skills to help clients feel safe and comfortable no matter the issue.

Exercise

There are circumstances that can sometimes interfere with one's ability to communicate verbally. Due to unfortunate events that remain overwhelming (for example, trauma, severe stress) even after conclusion of the event, the part of the brain responsible for physiological functioning (near the brain stem) can in fact become more active, leading to increased physiological arousal (i.e., stuttering, sweating, shaking, etc.). In turn, the frontal cortex can become inhibited or less active, contributing to disruptions in speech and thinking. If you have ever seen this or experienced it yourself, then you are aware of what this is like. This exercise is to help with these situations so that you or someone you know can experience a calming in your body so that if you choose to do so, you can talk more freely. This exercise can be completed with your therapist or with another person. You can also try it by yourself, but it may be challenging to focus on the sequence that follows.

To complete this exercise, please have the person who is helping you guide you through the following sequence and write down your responses in the spaces provided.

1. Ask the person to take a moment to think about a concern that he or she is currently facing that raises some level of emotional distress for him or her.

2. On a scale from 1 to 10, with 1 representing no distress at all and 10 representing overwhelming distress, what rating does the person give? _____

3. Write down any bodily sensations that the person may have at the moment.

_____

_____

_____

_____

4. Have the person take three deep breaths, inhaling and exhaling slowly. Encourage the person to focus only on his or her breathing.

5. Using a calm and quiet voice, say to the person, "I am with you and you are safe." Feel free to add in other things that may help the person to relax and settle down physiologically.

6. While continuing breathing at this rate, have the person notice how his or her body feels in its current position. If the person is uncomfortable, encourage him or her to move to a more comfortable place or position, if possible.

7. Suggest that the person notice his or her surroundings. Have the person look for something that increases his or her sense of peace. It could be a fixture, object, something natural, a color, or anything else that raises the level of calmness within.

8. Using the same scale as in Question #2, have the person rate his or her current level of distress.
   _____

9. If the level of distress is above a 4, repeat Steps 4 and 5. When the person achieves a 3 or below, ask him or her to share his or her current thoughts. Write down the person's responses below.

_____

_____

_____

_____

The point of this process is to help people who are feeling overwhelmed such that it affects their thinking and speaking, to become more relaxed and calm so that they can engage in conversation.

III.8   *Let It Be: Accepting What Is*

Therapist's Overview

Purpose of the Exercise

Events, situations, relationships, and happenings trigger an array of experiences within us. How we feel about things is never wrong; however, there are times when the voices of society tell us otherwise. Around us exist messages suggesting how we should or should not feel and experience the world. And yet, how we feel is never the problem. It is what we ultimately do that defines us. The purpose of this exercise is to connect with feelings and experiences and allow them to exist, devoid of explanations or attempts to rid ourselves of them. It is about accepting what we experience and allowing room for it within ourselves.

Suggestions for Use

1. This exercise can be used at any point in therapy.
2. We want to invite, not coerce or push people into talking about their feelings or experiences if they are uncomfortable with the proposition. As always, if a particular client is not interested in or declines an invitation to focus on internal experience, it is important to respect this preference. We only want to suggest that allowing internal experience to be present without judging it can be beneficial.

Exercise

How we feel things is always okay. No matter what messages, internal or external, attempt to nullify or dispute how we feel, we want to remind ourselves that all feelings and internal experiences are acceptable. We are not suggesting that all actions are acceptable. This exercise is to help you to connect with how you feel and to allow those experiences to exist within you, without judgment or having to explain yourself. To complete this exercise, please write your responses in the spaces provided.

1. Take a moment to reflect on the problem you are currently facing. Allow yourself to let whatever you experience thinking-wise, feeling-wise, and sensory-wise (visual, auditory, kinesthetically, etc.) to be present.

2. When you are ready, focus on the feelings and sensations you are experiencing. Focus on what you *feel* as opposed to what you think. Sit with that experience for as long as is right for you.

3. When you are ready, write down as many adjectives or descriptors that you can that describe what you experienced.

_____   _____

_____   _____

_____   _____

_____   _____

4. Reflecting on what you wrote, what do you notice?

_____

_____

_____

5. What, if any, messages do you recall that were either supportive of how you felt or challenged your experience?

_____

_____

_____

6. What do you notice when you cast away any messages of invalidation (i.e., "You shouldn't feel that way," "What's wrong with you?" or "That's stupid," etc.) and just allow your experiences to exist without judgment?

_____

_____

_____

7. How could you get yourself to cast aside external criticisms or challenges to your personal experience in the future?

_____

_____

_____

8. How could you get yourself to be a little more accepting and less critical of your personal experience in the future?

_____

_____

_____

From time to time it can be helpful to focus on your internal experiences and remember that what you feel is okay. When we make room in our experience internally we can be become more accepting of ourselves.

III.9   Let the Music Do the Talking: Sometimes Words Are Not Enough

Therapist's Overview

Purpose of the Exercise

Human beings have myriad forms of expression. At times, therapists can rely too heavily on their personal communication preferences that may limit possibilities for clients via other methods. It is a common truth that for many, music encapsulates a deeper emotional truth regarding shared experiences. As such, music has the ability to distill complex events and emotions to their core essence. This exercise is intended to facilitate a rich shared understanding between the client and clinician regarding the client's present concerns, future hopes, and potential roadblocks. The therapist can then assist the client in translating the experience into practical therapeutic application.

Suggestions for Use

1. This exercise can be used with individuals, groups, and families of all ages. It can be particularly helpful with clients who find verbal communication challenging or when multiple challenges present simultaneously.
2. Clinicians should refrain from offering any review or critique of the music. It is the subjective interpretation of the client that is solely valuable.

Exercise

At times, events in everyone's life feel as though they are too big and complex for words to fully encapsulate. Many then turn to that perfect song that seems to express exactly how they are feeling. This exercise is primarily a homework assignment. Take this sheet home with you and between now and the next time we meet, please find three songs. The first should describe how you are feeling about your situation right now. The second will focus on how your life will be when you are feeling better, and the last will describe what is standing between you and your goals. Remember, there are no right or wrong ways to choose a song, only what makes the most sense to you. After you find your songs, please take a few moments to respond to the questions below. If possible please bring your worksheet and the songs to our next session for discussion.

Song 1

1. What is the title of this song?

_____

2. When you hear this song, what comes to your mind?

_____

_____

3. How does this song make you feel?

_____

_____

4. What is the most important part of this song to you?

_____

_____

Song 2

1. What is the title of this song?

_____

2. How does this song reflect your positive vision of the future?

_____

_____

3. How does this song make you feel?

_____

_____

4. What is the most important element of this song to you?

_____

_____

Song 3

1. What is the title of this song?

_____

2. How does this song express what is keeping you from your vision of a positive future?

_____

_____

3. How does this song make you feel?

_____

_____

4. What is one thing you could do to face the challenges expressed in this song?

_____

_____

When you think about all of the songs you listed, collectively, what connections do you see?

_____

_____

_____

_____

What message can you take with you from the music you love that can inspire you when you most need it?

_____

_____

_____

_____

III.10   Using Positive Relationships to Enhance Positive Coping Mechanisms: Who Makes You Feel Good?

Therapist's Overview

Purpose of the Exercise

If the therapeutic relationship is an important factor that counselors and clients can build on to predict and influence positive outcomes, then it would stand to reason that examining existing positive relationships in clients' lives will help build positive change. Moreover, it would seem beneficial to examine what is a positive social relationship and to examine how these relationships are developed. Oftentimes, exploring affect around positive relationships is effective because most significant relationships are highly emotional. The purpose of this exercise is to examine positive social relationships as coping mechanisms to be utilized by your client to create and sustain change.

Suggestions for Use

1. This exercise can be utilized as a means to identify and amplify client strengths.
2. It may be used as a process statement with your client.
3. This exercise may be used as a mirror—how is this counseling relationship similar to or different than other relationships in your life.

Exercise

It could be most beneficial to introduce this exercise when the focus of the session is on interpersonal relationships or when discussing positive aspects of your client and how they can be transmitted to other areas of the client's life. Below are questions that can highlight how positive social relationships can be utilized to create change.

1. Think about important people in your life and what makes them important.

_____

_____

2. How did those relationships become so important?

_____

_____

3. If you had to describe those relationships as a feeling, what word(s) would come to mind?

_____

_____

4. How could you increase that feeling just a little bit?

_____

_____

5. If you were in a new relationship, how would you develop that feeling from scratch?

_____

_____

6. If you felt that feeling slip, how would you keep it from disappearing?

_____

_____

7. What role do you specifically play in creating and sustaining that feeling?

_____

_____

8. What role does your friend specifically play in creating and sustaining that feeling?

_____

_____

Here are a few additional suggestions to think about.

This exercise could also draw on the therapeutic relationship you developed with your client. You could ask your client, "What is it about our interactions that you find helpful?" This question would also serve as a process outcome rating. Additional follow-up questions could include the following:

1. How could you reproduce the positive interactions here in your everyday life?

_____

_____

2. When you start to interact differently with other people, who will be the first to notice?

_____

_____

3. What will that person say is different about your interactions?

_____

_____

III.11   Finding Meaning With Therapeutic Tattoos: Looking for Strengths in Unusual Places

Therapist's Overview

Purpose of the Exercise

Discussing client strengths is central to SSB therapies as a means to identify and amplify individual resources in the change process. Paralleling this idea are discussions with clients regarding their passions in life. Conversations focusing on passion often instill hope in their abilities and establish a foundation for continued change.

The purpose of this exercise is to allow clients to reconnect to their passions and to establish resources to meet their goals. Conversations centering on client passions will capitalize on client strengths and resources and ultimately focus on how the client can make changes in his or her life. This exercise may be useful once a therapeutic relationship has been established and when identifying client strengths.

Suggestions for Use

1. This exercise may be useful with older adolescents and adults; however, it can be used with younger children with slight modifications.
2. This exercise may help better understand from the client's perspective what he or she views as most meaningful in his or her life. (What is the client passionate about?)
3. It may help to capitalize on client passions and strengths and develop goals to meet the client's needs.
4. Cross-reference: Connect this exercise with any exercise on goal setting.

Exercise

Begin this exercise by asking your client if he or she was going to get a tattoo today, what would it be and why? You may have to set up the question by telling your client to like tattoos. (I learned this the hard way, the first two I times I attempted this exercise my clients did not like tattoos.) If you believe your clients would not respond to tattoos, you can ask if you were to buy a piece of artwork for your house, what would it be and what room would it go in? I do like the idea of the tattoo because it can be a permanent reminder of strengths.

Here are a few follow-up questions to ask after your client discusses his or her tattoo or artwork.

1. Summarize his or her response to focus on a key concept or experience. For example, a client discussing a palm tree, which could represent serenity.

_____

_____

_____

_____

2. Ask your client to scale how he or she is feeling regarding the key concept or experience. If you were to rate your serenity on a scale from 1 to 10, 10 being high in serenity, where are you currently? Write down his or her response(s).

Rating: _____

_____

_____

_____

_____

3. Continue with follow-up questions to address how your client could increase serenity in his or her life. What will be different in your life when are feeling more serene? Who would be the first person in your life to notice? What would he or she say is different about you?

_____

_____

_____

_____

4. Attempt to amplify areas in your client's life that he or she is satisfied with in regard to his or her key concept or experience.

5. Finally, develop a task assignment and have your client think about ways to increase his or her therapeutic tattoo and also discuss that tattoo in subsequent sessions as a process to monitor progress.

Task:

_____

_____

_____

_____

III.12   *The Oasis of the Mind: The Return of Memories Past*

Therapist's Overview

Purpose of the Exercise

Many clients experience their concerns primarily through the prism of emotion. As described in other exercises, there are times when verbal description may be insufficient to capture the totality of the nuances of a person's experiences. As overwhelming as emotional output may seem, everyone has in their history a memory that can provide comfort in the present day. The purpose of this exercise is for the therapist to guide the client through a visualization intended to help him or her identify memories and physical sensations that can be culled into present-day use.

Suggestions for Use

1. This exercise can be used with clients of any age.
2. It is optimal to use this visualization in an environment with as little outside sensory stimulation as possible.
3. This exercise can be used in conjunction with Exercise III.1, "Getting in Touch with Emotion: Hearing What Feelings Have to Say."

Exercise

Have you ever looked at an old photograph that made you smile? Pictures can be powerful reminders of the fun vacation, the surprise birthday party, or the big graduation. The mind is brimming with images from days past, but rather than call them photographs, they are referred to as memories. In difficult times, recalling a particular memory can provide comfort and reminders of what can be done today to return us to a more positive state of mind. This exercise is intended to lead you back to a particular time and place so that you may remember what has been of use to you in the past.

To complete this exercise, you first need only to listen. You may keep your eyes open, or close them, whatever you wish. Please get your body in a comfortable position. As questions are asked, you may choose to verbalize your answers or you may wish to write your answers on the worksheet when the visualization is complete.

Now, as we begin the visualization, I would like you to picture a time and place in which you felt good. It may have been fun, or calming. It may be in the recent past or something from a long time ago. There may be other people there, or you may be alone.

1. Where is the scene in your mind taking place?

_____

_____

_____

2. What do you see?

_____

_____

_____

3. Do you smell anything?

_____

_____

4. How does your body feel?

_____

_____

_____

5. Is there a particular temperature here?

_____

_____

_____

6. What sounds do you notice?

_____

_____

_____

7. What are you doing in this place?

_____

_____

_____

8. Is anyone there with you?

_____

_____

9. Is there anything more you would like to add to your visualization?

_____

_____

_____

As you leave this place, bringing your attention back to the room, realize that you can go back to this place any time you would like. You can stay as long as you wish, and it can be available to you as a place of comfort when life's challenges arise.

SECTION IV

EXPLORING NEW WORLDS OF POSSIBILITY
Changing Perspectives and Perceptions

IV.1 Life Pursuits and the Meaning of It All: Why Am I Here?

Therapist's Overview

Purpose of the Exercise

At one time or another, most people consider or ask questions of themselves to try and gain insight into the meaning of life. This can include asking, "Why am I here?" "What am I supposed to do with my life?" and so on. We often seek better understanding of our "life mission." The purpose of this exercise is to help you gain more meaning and understanding of your life in the present by considering key, future-oriented questions. These questions can help to pull clients toward the kinds of future they desire.

Suggestions for Use

1. This exercise is primarily for individuals, but with modification can be used with couples and families.
2. This exercise can be a meaningful exercise for adolescents, who are sometimes seen as being disinterested in the future.
3. This exercise can also help people to gain or rehabilitate a vision of the future.
4. If people struggle with specific questions, move past them to others. Some questions are more difficult to answer than others and yet most lead people to think.

Exercise

Beyond everyday questions such as, "What am I going to do today?" and "What's the point to all this?" are others that invite people to delve a little deeper. For those who may be more introspective, questions about the meaning of life, being, and existence come to mind with regularity. For those who may be less inclined to deliberately wonder about their existence, questions still arise from time to time. This exercise can help you to reflect on questions surrounding the meaning of life, make new connections, and set a course toward achieving the vision you created. To complete this exercise, follow the directions below.

1. Finding a Vision for the Future

   We first want to gain a sense of the future by asking ourselves questions that help us to better understand the meaning of life. Select one or more of the questions below, writing your answers in the spaces provided.

   What do you think is important for you to accomplish in the coming years?

   _____

   _____

   What dreams did you or do you have for yourself in upcoming days/weeks/months/years/life?

   _____

   _____

What are you here on the planet for?

_____

_____

What are human beings on the planet for, in your view?

_____

_____

What area do you think you could you make a contribution in?

_____

_____

What would you try to do with your life if you knew that you could not fail?

_____

_____

When you are finished, move to Number 2.

  2. Dealing With and Dissolving Barriers to the Preferred Future

  Sometimes we may be clear about what is meaningful to us but cannot get there because we perceive insurmountable barriers in our way. We have fears of success or fears of failure. They may include thinking we are inadequate to the task of making the dream happen or that certain things must happen before we begin to pursue our dreams. Answer one or more of the following questions that might prove helpful in clarifying these perceived barriers.

  What, in your view, stops you from getting to where you want to be with your life?

  _____

  _____

  What, in your view, stops you from realizing your dreams or getting to your goals?

  _____

  _____

  What do you believe must happen before you can realize your dreams/future?

  _____

  _____

What are the actions you have not taken to make your dreams and visions come true?

_____

_____

What things stand in your way of realizing your dreams and visions?

_____

_____

What would your heroes, models, or people you admire do if they were you in order to make this dream or vision happen?

_____

_____

What are you not doing, feeling, or thinking that they would in this situation?

_____

_____

What are you doing, feeling, or thinking that they would not?

_____

_____

Now, move on to Number 3.

3. Making an Action Plan to Reach the Preferred Future

Having a vision of the future and even realizing what the perceived barriers are will not necessarily make it happen. There must be a plan of action and a way to start to take some of those actions to make the future happen. Here are some ideas and questions that can help you to formulate and put into practice actions that will likely create their preferred futures. Please answer one or more of the following questions.

What could you do in the near future that would be steps toward getting you to where you want to be?

_____

_____

What could you do in the near future that would be steps toward realizing your visions and dreams?

_____

_____

What would be a first step toward realizing your dream/future?

_____

_____

What would you do as soon as you leave here?

_____

_____

What would you do tonight?

_____

_____

What would you be thinking that would help you take those steps?

_____

_____

Refer back to this exercise as needed to remind yourself of what is important to you and where you would like to be in your future. If you are in therapy, you might also consider sharing this with your therapist.

IV.2   *The Inner Limits: Interviewing Self for Solutions*

Therapist's Overview

Purpose of the Exercise

Problems have a way of distracting people from possibilities and solutions. It is clear, however, that most of the answers to our concerns ultimately come from within ourselves and our social systems. Sometimes, it is a matter of asking ourselves the kinds of questions that allow us to refocus our attention and access the resources to solve problems. The purpose of this exercise is to help people engage in self-interviews as a way of both finding solutions to present problems and preventing future problems.

Suggestions for Use

1. This exercise can be used at any point in therapy.
2. It can be helpful to work with clients to develop a series of questions or a checklist to follow that can help guide through self-interviews.
3. We do not want to suggest that there are formulaic answers or regimented procedures that will always work in the face of problems. Instead, our aim is to help clients to refocus their attention to internal and external resources.

Exercise

Therapy is a process that is largely based on the use of questioning. The right questions can trigger new emotions, ideas, and ways of viewing the world. Although therapy is often a catalyst to change, sometimes asking ourselves key questions can jumpstart positive change. This exercise can help you to develop a list of key questions that can be useful to you finding solutions to current and future concerns. To complete this exercise, please write your responses in the spaces provided.

Take a moment to reflect on a problem that you faced in the recent past and resolved. Next, consider the key questions that were asked of you or you asked of yourself that helped you either directly or indirectly to find solutions. List those questions below.

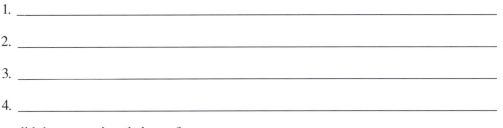

1. _____

2. _____

3. _____

4. _____

How did these questions help you?

_____

_____

_____

_____

Consider the current concern you are facing. Of the questions you listed previously, which ones are most applicable to this current concern?

1. _____

2. _____

3. _____

4. _____

What new questions might you add to this list?

1. _____

2. _____

3. _____

4. _____

If you knew someone who, in the future, was to face the same or a similar concern to the one you are facing now, what questions would you ask of him/her/them?

1. _____

2. _____

3. _____

4. _____

Create a list of key questions you came up with during this exercise and compose a list for future review.

1. _____

2. _____

3. _____

4. _____

5. _____

6. _____

7. _____

8. _____

IV.3   *What in the World? Noticing Between Session Change*

Therapist's Overview

Purpose of the Exercise

When people begin therapy, they often believe that the change they desire is going to happen in their sessions. Most change happens outside the therapeutic milieu and in everyday life. The purpose of this exercise is to orient clients to explore change that happens in between sessions to learn more about times when things are going better, problems are more manageable, and change seems to be happening in ways they prefer.

Suggestions for Use

1. This exercise can be used with individuals, couples, and families.
2. This exercise can be used at any point during therapy.
3. It can be helpful to remind clients that change is constant and to discuss with them examples of small change so they are not panning their lives for "all or nothing" moments.

Exercise

Therapy is an excellent avenue to further jumpstart change when we are stuck. At the same time, most of the change we experience happens outside of therapy and in our everyday lives. If we are looking for it, we will find moments when things are going more the way we would like and, in fact, perhaps much better than we anticipated. There are moments when the problems that have held us captive are less dominating and disruptive. This exercise can help you to identify these moments as they happen in between sessions. You can then build on them on your own and discuss them with your therapist. To complete this exercise, please follow the directions listed, answering any questions below by writing your answers in the spaces provided.

1. In between your scheduled therapy visits, focus on the following thought: *I am going to notice things happening in my life that I would like to have continue.*

   Consider how you might remind yourself to focus on this thought. Write down one way you might do this.

   _____

   _____

2. During the time between meetings with your therapist, consider the small things that happen from minute to minute, hour to hour, and day to day. Notice the things that make your life just a little easier and your day just a little better or brighter. They may be things that make you smile or temporarily give you relief. As you notice things happen, write them down in the spaces below. Be specific, noting what happened, when it happened, what were the conditions, how long it lasted, and who else might have been around.

   a. _____

   _____

b. _____

_____

_____

c. _____

_____

_____

3. Now, in general, what did you notice about the things you wrote down for the previous answer?

_____

_____

_____

4. How is that or could it be helpful to you?

_____

_____

_____

5. How can you build on those small moments to expand them in your life and get them to happen a little more often?

_____

_____

_____

Continue this exercise and you might find that you more automatically begin to notice the influence you have over your concerns and how change that happens every day can be meaningful in your life.

IV.4   *Pollyanna Grows Up: From Positives to Strengths*

Therapist's Overview

Purpose of the Exercise

A common misconception about strengths and solution-based (SSB) therapies is that they are primarily about being positive or "looking on the bright side." This perception can have negative unintended consequences. Clients entering a therapist's office for the first time bring with them concerns and challenges that are very real, and a "Pollyanna" response can leave them feeling unheard and invalidated. The purpose of this exercise is to practice the emphasis of client strengths while at the same time avoiding descriptions that ignore or minimize presenting concerns. By becoming proficient in this artful use of language, clinicians can better ensure successful engagement with the client and establish possibilities for the achievement of goals and outcomes.

Suggestions for Use

1. This exercise is intended for therapists who are interested in honing their use of SSB language and assessment.
2. Supervision can be an effective venue for this activity for therapists working with clients presenting with multiple concerns.
3. Cross-reference: This exercise can be augmented with the use of Exercise II.8, "G-O! Focusing on Goals and Outcomes."

Exercise

During the therapeutic process, a clinician wears many hats. From cheerleader to teacher, mentor to confidante, a therapist will be asked to match the concerns of a client that may change from moment to moment. Regardless of the task at hand, however, it is crucial that the therapist maintain a perspective and use of language that is strengths and solution based rather than simply positive. This distinction is key, as it, in part, differentiates the professional helper from the trusted friend or sympathetic ear. To complete the exercise, read the below scenarios and answer the questions that follow.

Scenario 1

Jake is a 35-year-old single father of two. Despite carrying two jobs, Jake is on the verge of losing his home and health insurance. This is of particular concern to Jake because one of his children has a chronic illness that requires constant monitoring and care. He initiated services because he reports feeling depressed, having trouble sleeping, and experiencing periodic anxiety attacks. In addition, Jake recently ended a two-year relationship after his partner took a job in another state.

1. What strengths do you identify in Jake?

_____

_____

_____

2. How can Jake build on these strengths to address his presenting concerns?

_____

_____

_____

3. How would Pollyanna look at Jake's situation?

_____

_____

_____

4. How could this outlook hinder collaboration with Jake?

_____

_____

_____

Scenario 2

Beth is a 16-year-old female who was referred to counseling by her mother. After her parents' divorce, Beth began acting out verbally and physically toward her younger brother. Most of the outbursts occur when Beth cares for her sibling after school while her mother is at work. Although previously on the school honor roll, Beth's grades have dropped during the current semester, and she runs the risk of removal from the school swimming team. Beth reports that she speaks infrequently with her father but wonders if she can soon live with him.

1. What strengths do you identify in Beth?

_____

_____

_____

2. How can Beth build on these strengths to address her presenting concerns?

_____

_____

_____

3. How would Pollyanna look at Beth's situation?

_____

_____

_____

4. How could this outlook hinder collaboration with Beth?

_____

_____

_____

Scenario 3

Maggie is a 53-year-old corporate executive with one grown daughter and two grandchildren. Following the death of her husband nine months ago, Maggie reports difficulty focusing, spontaneous crying spells, and frequent insomnia. She also states that her productivity at work is declining, and she no longer participates in her book club. Maggie says that she has three close friends who check in on her often by phone, but that she is finding herself beginning to withdraw.

1. What strengths do you identify in Maggie?

_____

_____

_____

2. How can Maggie build on these strengths to address her presenting concerns?

_____

_____

_____

3. How would Pollyanna look at Maggie's situation?

_____

_____

_____

4. How could this outlook hinder collaboration with Maggie?

_____

_____

_____

IV.5 *The Art of the Frame: Using Reality-Defining Language*

Therapist's Overview

Purpose of the Exercise

When making the evolution toward strengths and solution-focused therapy, language is often the most powerful tool in transforming deficits to assets. The frame by which clients describe themselves and therapists conceptualize situations can be the difference between hopelessness and possibility. This exercise is intended to provide the therapist with the opportunity to practice framing some of the most commonly heard negative statements into ones that can shape a therapeutic conversation toward solutions and strengths. Identifying these critical statements can orient the client in a way that yields a broader contextual understanding and possibility for future movement.

Suggestions for Use

1. This exercise can be used individually or during supervision with therapists.
2. This exercise can be adapted for clinical use in group or family settings.
3. Cross-reference: This exercise can be used together with Exercise VII.1, "The Reflective Consultation: A Conversational Approach to Generating Change."

Exercise

When carrying on strengths-based assessments or conversations, the effectiveness of the conversation will partly be determined by the manner in which a concern, characteristic, or behavior is defined. A "headstrong" client to one person is "opinionated" to another. With an alteration of language, "hyperactive" becomes "energetic." A successful reframe is one that does not discount a client's subjective experience but adds perspective in such a way that additional potential for change comes into focus. Below are a series of statements along with space to practice reframing them. Remember, a single statement has the possibility of multiple redefinitions, so write as many as possible for each statement.

1. "He doesn't do his chores on time."

    Reframe: _____

    _____

    _____

2. "She is always smothering me."

    Reframe: _____

    _____

    _____

3. "I don't get to do what I want."

   Reframe: _____

   _____

   _____

4. "I worry about everything."

   Reframe: _____

   _____

   _____

5. "I never seem to have enough time."

   Reframe: _____

   _____

   _____

6. "Her anger is uncontrollable."

   Reframe: _____

   _____

   _____

7. "Why does this keep happening to me?"

   Reframe: _____

   _____

   _____

8. "I'm tired of fighting."

   Reframe: _____

   _____

   _____

9. "His grades are terrible."

    Reframe: _____

    _____

    _____

10. "I wish I didn't cry all the time."

    Reframe: _____

    _____

    _____

Which reframe was most difficult for you? What made it most difficult?

_____

_____

_____

Which reframe was the easiest for you? What made it easiest?

_____

_____

_____

IV.6   Completing the Puzzle of Your Life: Putting the Pieces Together

Therapist's Overview

Purpose of the Exercise

SSB therapy and other constructivist approaches are very concerned with how the individual views his or her complaint and ideas of change. Engaging clients in this process early can lead to higher levels of self-efficacy, a heightened sense of their strengths, and a strong therapeutic relationship. Discussing with your clients how they view their self, strengths, and theory of change is one way to accomplish the above.

The value of this exercise is to have clients think about their selves and complaints in a different fashion. Asking your client to describe his or her life in terms of a life puzzle can be another way for your client to visualize his or her strengths, complaint, and means for change. This exercise can be used early on in a session or when a new complaint is presented.

Suggestions for Use

1. Adults and adolescents are developmentally appropriate for this exercise.
2. This exercise may be used to allow a better opportunity for clients to identify their strengths.
3. This exercise may be used when talking with clients to help them reveal how they view their self.
4. Connecting this exercise with Exercise III.11, "Finding Meaning With Therapeutic Tattoos: Looking for Strengths in Unusual Places," may give a picture to the puzzle and increase its effectiveness.

Exercise

To begin this exercise, ask your client to describe his or her understanding of his or her self as a puzzle: Right now, if your life was a puzzle, what would it look like? Careful attending to your client's response can give you information on his or her readiness to change and his or her strengths. If your client describes his or her life puzzle as in a box sitting on a self, your client is probably very early on in his or her change process. If your client states his or her life puzzle has its border and the beginning of the center section, perhaps he or she has a good sense of his or her self and is working toward maintaining and amplifying his or her change. To complete this exercises, consider the following questions and write your responses in the spaces provided.

1. What needs to happen to put another piece of your life puzzle together?

_____

_____

_____

_____

2. Now that you have more of your life puzzle together, what are you accomplishing that you were not before?

_____

_____

_____

_____

3. If another person was helping you with your puzzle, who would it be? How would that person complement your strengths?

_____

_____

_____

_____

4. When ending a session, you could ask your client to notice over the next week how he or she puts pieces of his or her life puzzle together with ease—similar to a first session task.

_____

_____

_____

_____

When starting the next session, consider asking your client, "How much of your life puzzle do you have together?" Stating your question as a positive will presuppose change.

IV.7   *My Biography: In Your Own Words*

Therapist's Overview

Purpose of the Exercise

One way to think about life is as an evolving story or narrative with twists and turns, ups and downs, and plenty of changes along the way. The purpose of this exercise is to help clients to explore their life narratives and document the changes they experienced. Through this process, it is hoped that clients will better appreciate their efforts, strengths, resiliencies, and how they faced up to challenges both large and small. In addition, we can encourage clients to continue to actively employ strategies that will further encourage possibilities for the future.

Suggestions for Use

1. This exercise is primarily for individuals. It can also be used with couples and families. To do this, it is suggested that the couple or family create a unified narrative that is reflective of that couple or family's story.
2. If a person becomes stuck or has trouble with some aspect of the exercise, he or she can bypass that section and move to another.

Exercise

Consider your life as one evolving story that covers all aspects of the good, the bad, and the ugly. Because we do not always take time to reflect on how our lives unfolded, we sometimes miss some really great parts and, in some instances, what we learned during the challenges we faced. The purpose of this exercise is to explore various aspects of our life stories or narratives and reflect on where we have been, what we learned, and where we are going. To complete this exercise, please respond to the prompts below by writing your answers in the spaces provided.

The first years of my life can best be described as

_____ .

Over time I realized that I _____

and that I _____ .

I was able to deal with the challenges I faced by _____ .

My main sources of support were _____

who helped me by _____ .

As I got a little older, it became clearer to me that I_____

_____ .

This helped me to _____ .

What I know about myself is that I _____ .

With this self-knowledge, I now can _____ .

So each day I try to _____ .

In the coming days or months, I will _____ .

When I face some form of adversity, I will _____

_____ .

I will also remain aware of what has helped me in the past and how that could help me in the future

by _____

_____ .

As my life continues to evolve, I will be sure to remember that I am _____

_____ .

I will also remember that my life story, as it is written now, will continue to grow and change, which

I see as _____

_____ .

Please take some time to reflect on what you have written. You might also consider sharing it with others.

IV.8   *20,000 to 1: It Takes Only One*

Therapist's Overview

Purpose of the Exercise

Most of the change clients will experience occurs outside of therapy. In fact, some estimate that there are as many as 20,000 moments in a given day by which a person's life can be positively impacted. This means that there are numerous opportunities each day for people to reap positive benefits of what may initially appear as small, insignificant moments. By identifying small moments and occurrences, people can begin to notice that there are exceptions to problems and things are not always as they seem at first glance. We can then work with a client to build on these small moments. The purpose of this exercise is to engage clients in ways of shifting their attention to small exceptions to their concerns and problems as opposed to waiting only for large, sweeping ones. It takes only one exception to introduce possibilities into otherwise closed-down situations.

Suggestions for Use

1. This exercise can be used at any point in therapy.
2. It can be helpful to discuss the concept of "exceptions," times when problems are less intrusive, more manageable, or absent altogether.
3. Cross-reference: See Exercise II.7, "What Does That Look Like? Translating Ambiguity Through Action-Talk."

Exercise

In the face of problems, it is easy to become focused on finding big, sweeping changes. Most change, however, tends to come in small moments and doses. They are the kinds of moments that if you are not looking for them, you are likely to miss them. The good news is that in any given day, there are typically many exceptions, times when things go differently, if only slightly, regarding problems. In other words, problems tend to exist on a continuum from very bad to nonexistent. We are not looking for all or nothing here, just those moments when things go or have gone a little differently. This exercise will help you to identify and build on those moments. To complete this exercise, follow the instructions below and then write your answers in the spaces provided.

1. Prior to starting your day, write down the concern you are most worried about. Be sure to use action-talk to describe the concern. Please write that concern in the spaces below.

_____

_____

_____

_____

2. On a scale of 1 to 10, with 1 representing "very present" to 10 representing "not present at all," rate the current "presence" of your concern. _____

3. Next, using the following grid, over the course of a 24-hour period, rate the presence of the concern in your life during each period of time. In the adjacent column, for any number of 6 or higher, write what was different about that time frame that may have made the problem seem to be more manageable or made it seem that things were better.

Time of Day	"Presence" Rating	For Score of 6 or Higher, What Was Different?
6:00 a.m.–7:00 a.m.		
7:00 a.m.–8:00 a.m.		
9:00 a.m.–10:00 a.m.		
10:00 a.m.–11:00 a.m.		
11:00 a.m.–12:00 p.m.		
12:00 p.m.–1:00 p.m.		
1:00 p.m.–2:00 p.m.		
2:00 p.m.–3:00 p.m.		
3:00 p.m.–4:00 p.m.		
4:00 p.m.–5:00 p.m.		
5:00 p.m.–6:00 p.m.		
6:00 p.m.–7:00 p.m.		
7:00 p.m.–8:00 p.m.		
8:00 p.m.–9:00 p.m.		
9:00 p.m.–10:00 p.m.		
10:00 p.m.–11:00 p.m.		
11:00 p.m.–12:00 a.m.		
12:00 a.m.–1:00 a.m.		
1:00 a.m.–2:00 a.m.		
2:00 a.m.–3:00 a.m.		
3:00 a.m.–4:00 a.m.		
4:00 a.m.–5:00 a.m.		
5:00 a.m.–6:00 a.m.		

4. Looking over the grid from the 24-hour period you tracked, what do you notice about the scores that were 6 or higher?

_____

_____

_____

_____

5. List the things you did differently during the times when things were better.

   a. _____

   b. _____

   c. _____

   d. _____

   e. _____

6. What, if anything, did you learn about the effect a small change can have?

_____

_____

_____

_____

7. What can you do with this information?

_____

_____

_____

_____

IV.9   *Dear Diary: What Were My Strengths Today?*

Therapist's Overview

Purpose of the Exercise

A common piece of therapeutic homework is to ask a client to keep a log or a diary detailing specific pieces of information. Sometimes, we, as clinicians, forget that this type of activity need not only be useful for those with whom we work. It may also yield valuable information for ourselves. The intent of this exercise is to help the therapist identify his or her areas of strength that are present every day. With careful examination, the therapist will see how even the most seemingly fleeting thoughts, acts, and attitudes can be viewed as representing strengths that can be augmented in other areas of their lives. The development of this skill is at the core of becoming an effective strengths and solution-focused therapist.

Suggestions for Use

1. This activity is intended for clinicians who are beginning to familiarize themselves with SSB therapy.
2. The activity can easily be modified for use with individual clients of all ages.
3. This activity may be a useful supervision tool for supervisors who wish to expand the skill set of a supervisee.
4. Larger trends will be discovered if the exercise is repeated multiple times.
5. Cross-references: This exercise can be used along with Exercise I.6, "Me, Myself, and I: Understanding Personal Strengths" and Exercise VII.1, "The Reflective Consultation: A Conversational Approach to Generating Change."

Exercise

An individual's strengths are not only reflected in that person's overall outlook on life, themselves, and others. When closely sought, strengths are found in the actions we all take every day but often do not take the time to notice. Strengths are found in many places, from the random gesture of kindness offered to a stranger, to the telephone call made to a sick friend. Below is a series of statements that invite you to notice and appreciate the strengths you utilize everyday. Identifying strengths is a skill. With practice, you should be better able to do for others what these questions encourage you to do for yourself.

Date: _____

1. Today's following thoughts and actions are those of which I am most proud:

_____

_____

_____

2. The following describes what those thoughts and actions say about my strengths:

_____

_____

_____

3. One challenge I faced today was:

_____

_____

_____

4. The following describes how my strengths can help me meet this challenge in the future:

_____

_____

_____

IV.10   *Life Witnesses: Meaningful Connections and Enduring Relationships*

Therapist's Overview

Purpose of the Exercise

All of us face difficulty from time to time. During these times, it is important to seek the help of others for acknowledgment, validation, and support. Sometimes we just need someone to listen. One of the ways we are able to cope with our pain and suffering is through the help of others. In fact, if you ask most people, they will identify at least one person who made a difference in their lives at one point or another. We refer to such persons as "life witnesses." By identifying such persons, we can reorient clients to times when they felt acknowledged and understood, when they accessed past resources and tapped into previous solutions to problems. This exercise is designed to help people identify current and past persons and relationships that helped them through difficult times. Once these relationships are identified, we can help others determine how those relationships were helpful to them and how that might assist them with coping better with their concern and life situations.

Suggestions for Use

1. Even though we are asking people to recall past relationships, it is not necessary for the person who helped out to be available in the present. What we want to know is how the relationship helped the client (e.g., if a client said, "I really wish my sister were around, she understood me"). Although we cannot bring back a deceased loved one, we can ask, "What was it about your relationship with your sister that helped you through times of trouble?" We then find out that the person felt heard and understood. We can then follow with, "So when you feel heard and understood what happens for you?"
2. Some people will think of many persons who helped them out, and others will struggle to identify just one. Therefore, it can sometimes be helpful to go through different scenes of their lives and ask them to identify significant people during those times. We can then ask, "Tell about the role that _____ played in your life at that time."

Exercise

As social beings, relationships and connections to others are essential. This does not mean that we always have to want to be around people, just that having a shoulder to lean on or someone to listen can make all the difference for us when we are facing life struggles. These persons can be family members, friends, teachers, coaches, or scout leaders. Over the course of life, most people can identify a person or several people who were there for them in times of trouble, helped them to solve problems, get through difficult times, and for some, helped them to stay alive. This exercise will help you to identify those life witnesses who made a difference in your life in the past. It is not necessary for those people to still be around. Oftentimes just reminding ourselves of what we gained from our relationships with such persons is enough to get us back on track. To complete this exercise, write down your responses in the spaces provided.

1. Think back to a time when you felt most connected to this person or those persons. What was it about that person or those persons that contributed to your sense of connection?

_____

_____

2. Whom have you met in your life who would understand exactly what you have been going through?

_____

_____

_____

3. How is it helpful for you to know that this person or those persons would understand?

_____

_____

_____

4. If you could speak with that person, what would he or she suggest that you do?

_____

_____

_____

5. When things were going better for you than they have been, who was around to help you out and make a difference in your life?

_____

_____

_____

6. What did that person say or do?

_____

_____

_____

7. How was that helpful to you?

_____

_____

_____

8. If he or she were here, what might that person suggest to you to help with what you have been going through?

_____

_____

_____

9. What would it take for you to follow that suggestion a little bit now?

_____

_____

_____

In addition to what you have written down, consider how you might connect further or reconnect with someone who has been a support to you in the past.

IV.11   Gratitudes: Appreciating Others

Therapist's Overview

Purpose of the Exercise

There is an old saying, "Give and you shall receive." There are many reasons to give and help others. A wonderful benefit of giving is the joy that it can bring to those who give. Gifts, often in the form of small gestures, can be especially meaningful. They can strengthen connections and contribute to the lives of others. The purpose of this exercise is to help clients recognize how small expressions of appreciation and gratitude can benefit others as well as the clients themselves.

Suggestions for Use

1. This exercise can be used with individuals, couples, or families.
2. This exercise can be used for people in or out of therapy.
3. Clients should be encouraged to be creative in their giving. The importance of giving is in the intent and gesture and not in the gift itself.
4. Remember that there are many ways to let others know how we feel. Keep your expressions small, yet personal. Do not do it because you have to. Do it because it matters to you and to the others who experience the gift of your caring.

Exercise

Many are familiar with the saying, "The gift is in the giving." When we are experiencing pain or suffering, however, one of the last things we might think of doing is giving to others. There are times when we may not even feel that we have the energy to expend on giving. And yet, that is the paradox. By giving, we often open ourselves up in new ways. We reconnect with ourselves and others. One of the simplest forms of giving is by acknowledging others and expressing gratitude. This exercise can help you to let others know how you feel about them and in the process do something very nice for yourself. This can even help you to experience and see the world anew. To complete this exercise, write your responses to the questions in the spaces provided.

1. What is a small thing that someone has done for you that let you know he or she cared about you?

_____

_____

_____

_____

_____

2. What was most meaningful about that act or gift?

_____

_____

_____

_____

3. Make a list of persons you are grateful for in your life.

_____   _____

_____   _____

_____   _____

_____   _____

_____   _____

_____   _____

4. What are three different ways that you could let one or more of those persons know how much you appreciate them?

a. _____

_____

b. _____

_____

c. _____

_____

5. What would it take for you to express your gratitude to one or more of the persons you listed within the next week?

_____

_____

_____

_____

6. Over the next week, express your gratitude to one or more persons. Then write down what it was like for you to give to others. Note your thoughts and feelings.

IV.12   *Vantage Point: Multiple Angles, Multiple Solutions*

Therapist's Overview

Purpose of the Exercise

Any event or object looks very different when viewed from different angles. A client who is over-whelmed by life circumstances may become mired in a single perspective that can obscure alterna-tive available possibilities. By asking the client to take on the vantage points of significant others in their lives, new understandings can emerge that illuminate hidden resources. Even though complete understanding of another vantage point may not be possible, even a cursory attempt may be nonethe-less fruitful. The thrust of this exercise is to engage the client in a conversation that compares and contrasts his or her individual perceptions and actions with those who may also have a stake in the situation. The point, of course, is not to invalidate the client's perspective, only to explore the pos-sibility that others may have valuable insight to offer.

Suggestions for Use

1. This activity is intended for adult clients with multiple stakeholders in their lives.
2. Cross-reference: This activity may be presented with Exercise II.16, "The Spokes of Life: Cultivating Resources."

Exercise

My mother has an opinion on just about everything, and she is not afraid to share it. If she feels someone could use a haircut, he or she will know it. If an important decision is to be made, she will be the first in line to place her vote. When life presents its struggles, my mother will have thought about it long and hard. It can be helpful when times are hard to hear the opinions of the important people in our lives. This activity will help us articulate the way others may be thinking of your cur-rent situation. Of course, the most important point of view is yours, but by filling in the spaces below, we may find some possibilities for change that have not yet been considered.

Your Perspective

Your Name: _____

1. What significant concern or challenge are you currently facing?

_____

_____

_____

_____

2. On a scale of 1 to 10, with 10 being the most severe, how concerning or difficult is this challenge?

_____

3. What have you tried in the past to address this concern or challenge?

_____

4. What would you like to try in the future?

_____

Your Best Friend's Perspective

Your Best Friend's Name: _____

1. What significant concern or challenge is your friend currently facing?

_____

_____

_____

_____

2. On a scale of 1 to 10, with 10 being the most severe, how concerning or difficult is this challenge?

_____

3. What has your friend tried in the past to address this concern or challenge?

_____

4. What do you think your friend should try in the future?

_____

Your Significant Other's Perspective

Your Significant Other's Name: _____

1. What significant concern or challenge is your partner currently facing?

_____

_____

_____

2. On a scale of 1 to 10, with 10 being the most severe, how concerning or difficult is this challenge?

_____

3. What has your partner tried in the past to address this concern or challenge?

_____

4. What do you think your partner should try in the future?

_____

Your Boss or Coworker's Perspective

Your Boss or Coworker's Name: _____

1. What significant concern or challenge is your employee or coworker currently facing?

_____

_____

_____

_____

2. On a scale of 1 to 10, with 10 being the most severe, how concerning or difficult is this challenge?

_____

3. What has your employee or coworker tried in the past to address this concern or challenge?

_____

4. What do you think your employee or coworker should try in the future?

_____

Additional Significant Person's Perspective

Your Significant Person's Name: _____

1. What significant concern or challenge is this person in your life currently facing?

_____

_____

_____

_____

2. On a scale of 1 to 10, with 10 being the most severe, how concerning or difficult is this challenge?

_____

3. What has this person tried in the past to address this concern or challenge?

_____

4. What do you think this person should try in the future?

_____

Which, if any, of your responses surprised you? What did you learn or perhaps had you not thought of before?

_____

_____

_____

_____

Consider sharing your responses with those you spoke for above. Compare their actual answers with those you anticipated.

IV.13   *History Is Now: The Wisdom of Others*

Therapist's Overview

Purpose of the Exercise

The path that brings individuals to the study and practice of therapy is always filled with inspirational experiences, relationships, and events. Along the way, ideas and philosophies are culled from sources as varied and as personal as each individual's story. Given the hectic cacophony of modern life, it is rare that time and homage are given to those who have gone before us who provided invaluable insight and learning. This exercise is intended to provide the opportunity to note the teachers, artists, scientists, family members, and leaders whose words and deeds help inform who we are today. By codifying their individual meaning to us, more precise insight can be discovered about how we view ourselves, our clients, and the work we do.

Suggestions for Use

1. This exercise is suggested for any practitioner seeking to gain a greater understanding of his or her worldview.
2. This exercise may also be a helpful tool during supervision as a teaching tool for novice therapists.
3. Cross-reference: This exercise can also be used in conjunction with Exercise I.1, "The Philosophical Inventory: Expanding Awareness and Impact of Beliefs" and Exercise I.5, "Composing Your Theoretical Worldview: What I Believe."

Exercise

If a person's life is seen as an unfolding story, everyone has many contributing editors. Although maintaining a future focus is critical in our work with our clients and our individual personal and professional development, it can be instructive to take note of those people in our past who provided instruction, inspiration, and modeling. These important leaders in our lives may have provided their guidance through words, actions, personal interactions, or great achievement. The possibilities are endless. Most important is their impact on your growth and learning. Space is provided below to identify these individuals and to reflect on their continuing influence on your life and your work.

Inspiration: _____

1. What he or she said or did:

_____

_____

2. This impacted me by:

_____

_____

3. This person influences my work by:

_____

_____

_____

4. I am most like this person when:

_____

_____

_____

5. If there were one word to describe this person, it would be:

_____

Inspiration: _____

1. What he or she said or did:

_____

_____

_____

2. This impacted me by:

_____

_____

_____

3. This person influences my work by:

_____

_____

_____

4. I am most like this person when:

_____

_____

_____

5. If there were one word to describe this person, it would be:

_____

Inspiration: _____

1. What he or she said or did:

_____

_____

_____

2. This impacted me by:

_____

_____

_____

3. This person influences my work by:

_____

_____

_____

4. I am most like this person when:

_____

_____

_____

5. If there were one word to describe this person, it would be:

_____

IV.14   The Road Less Traveled: Exploring the Hidden Possibilities During Life's Most Challenging Times

Therapist's Overview

Purpose of the Exercise

Robert Frost wrote, "two roads diverged in the woods and I, I took the one less traveled by—and that has made all the difference." Sometimes clients get mired in continuing down familiar, if ineffective, paths even when other alternatives are present. This is often due to the tendency for familiarity to obscure alternative approaches.

This exercise can be used at any point during the process where an unhelpful pattern of behavior or interaction seems intractable. It can be helpful in assisting the client to identify various approaches to situations that ease the accomplishment of their goals.

Suggestions for Use

1. This exercise can be used with children, adolescents, adults, and groups.
2. Descriptions of difficult situations should be encouraged to be as specific and concrete as possible, paying attention to both the facts of the story as well as the client's subjective experience of the event.
3. It is beneficial for the therapist to encourage the development of multiple points of divergence as well as possible solutions.
4. The exercise should be used to explore a single discrete incident that may exemplify a larger pattern.

Exercise

In every situation, even one in which we feel like we have no control, there are key points during which if something different happened, even if it is very small, the outcome would have been changed radically. This exercise is going to help you identify one or more of those crossroads in this situation as well as give you some ideas about how to modify your response in the future to give you the outcome you want.

- Please make yourself as comfortable as possible. Now imagine yourself walking into the room where the incident took place. Please describe what you see, hear, and smell. What are you thinking in this scenario? How would you rate this situation now on a scale of 1 to 10 with 10 being the worst this story will get?

Rating: _____

- Now, continue on with the story, continuing to notice and describe both what is going on around you and what you are thinking and feeling. When the scene reaches the point of maximum intensity, please pause and let me know.

Rating: _____

Since you identified the moment that was most troublesome to you, I would like us to take a few minutes to answer some questions.

1. Please rewind the story in your mind and identify the point at which things seemed to begin deteriorating.

_____

_____

_____

2. What were the key actions or events that led to this change in direction?

_____

_____

_____

3. What are two or three actions you could have taken at this point that could have led to a different outcome?

_____

_____

_____

4. Which of these actions would be easiest for you to take in the future?

_____

_____

_____

5. How do you imagine you would rate the situation if these actions were taken?

_____

_____

_____

IV.15 Being the Author of Your Life: Say What You Need to Say

Therapist's Overview

Purpose of the Exercise

Collaborating with clients on envisioning their preferred future is a key concept in most SSB questioning techniques. "Being the Author of Your Life" is another variation of that model. When clients can think about their futures in different terms or from other perspectives, it can facilitate change and procedures to put their change in motion. "Being the Author of Your Life" is similar to the miracle question where clients engage creative thinking and goal setting as a result of envisioning their future in a unique perspective. As a result, clients will be able to have a new view of their complaint from affective, cognitive, and behavioral perspectives. Collaborating with your clients on their new view of their complaint, the clients may be able to "see" the change they are making, facilitate and sustain future change, and begin to envision what their world will be like when they no longer need to continue counseling.

Suggestions for Use

1. Clients in any stage of counseling can benefit from this exercise.
2. This exercise may work well with clients who enjoy reading or who are global thinkers.
3. This exercise can be utilized with clients when they are in a transition to enable them to envision and plan for the future.

Exercise

Once you believe your client is in a position to benefit from this exercise (as a summary statement, transition in topic, to highlight change that has occurred), simply ask your client to envision his or her life as a book. Here are additional questions you could use to follow up.

1. If your life was a book, what chapter would it be in?

_____

_____

2. What kind of book would it be—science fiction, mystery, or romance?

_____

_____

3. After reading your book, how would you feel and what would you have learned?

_____

_____

4. If it were a biography, who would be the author?

_____

_____

5. What would be the title of your book if you wrote it?

_____

_____

6. Who would be the first person to read your book?

_____

_____

7. How does the book end?

_____

_____

8. What steps need to be completed to finish your book?

a. _____

_____

b. _____

_____

c. _____

_____

9. What steps have you taken to complete your book?

a. _____

_____

b. _____

_____

c. _____

_____

10. If you were to give the book to someone, who would it be?

_____

_____

11. If you were to write an inscription, what would it say?

_____

_____

12. If your book was successful and came out in a second edition, what would be added?

_____

_____

IV.16   *More on Meeting Yourself Again: Living With Yourself*

Therapist's Overview

Purpose of the Exercise

Acknowledging client abilities and a shift in focus from deficits to strengths is a necessary step for clients to relearn who they are. The purpose of this exercise is to go beyond examining client strengths to further gain an awareness of the client's new self. In addition to clients' recognizing their resources, clients' having a realistic understanding of their environment will provide the opportunity for effective change. This focus is extremely beneficial when discussing activities of daily living. It is one thing to know someone has the interest or ability to "do" a certain job, but it is also just as important to know how his or her environment and history impact securing employment. For example, how does securing employment change for a qualified person who has a felony or disability?

This exercise will specifically examine how the client can be realistic about his or her environment and still maintain change. When clients acknowledge resources and strengths and are also realistic about their abilities and environment, they will have a better understanding of who they are and hopefully begin to assess their self value against internal goals that are meaningful to them.

Suggestions for Use

1. This exercise may be useful as a follow-up to the identification of client strengths.
2. Older adolescents and adults can benefit from this exercise.
3. This exercise will explore affect and emotion of your client's new self.
4. This exercise may also be helpful to clients who are analytic or those who could benefit from additional organizational development.
5. Cross-reference: This exercise may be used in conjunction with Exercise II.2, "Hello My Name Is: Meeting Yourself Again."

Exercise

It will be most beneficial to begin this exercise when your client is discussing a specific activity of daily living (i.e., employment, transportation, education, housing, budgeting) or when beginning the goal-setting process. The following questions can be used to facilitate the process.

1. What do you have at your disposal that allows you to "do" this job (or another activity of daily living)?

_____

_____

2. What other aspects of your life do you need to be aware of (education, child care, transportation, etc.) to secure and maintain employment?

_____

_____

3. What can you do on your own to help get organized to secure employment?

_____

_____

4. What aspects of your life could you use a little help in to get organized to secure employment?

_____

_____

5. Once you secure employment (or another activity of daily living), what will you need to do to maintain employment?

_____

_____

6. Are there resources at your place of employment that you will need to access to maintain and thrive at your job?

_____

_____

7. How will you envision your view of yourself after you are working for a week, month, and year?

_____

_____

SECTION V

LIVES IN MOTION
Changing Patterns of Action and Interaction

V.1   Getting Off the Hamster Wheel: Going Forward With Purpose

Therapist's Overview

Purpose of the Exercise

When many clients enter therapy, they express what they see as a negative situation repeating itself time after time after time. The seemingly intractable nature of these cycles can lead to a loss of hope and the perpetuation of a difficult cycle. By stepping out of the cycle, sometimes in subtle ways, the client may discover potentialities that were hidden while they ran breathlessly inside the hamster wheel. To be effective at this exercise, the therapist ideally should have a keen eye for detail as well as a fearlessness in offering suggestions that may appear unconventional.

Suggestions for Use

1. This exercise is best used later in the course of therapy after the therapeutic alliance has had an opportunity to mature.
2. This exercise is intended for clients who report feeling "stuck" or who express difficulty generating alternative possibilities for addressing their concerns.
3. Cross-references: Can be effective used in addition to Exercise IV.14, "The Road Less Traveled: Exploring the Hidden Possibilities During Life's Most Challenging Times."

Exercise

After many attempts at trying to solve some of life's most difficult challenges, some people throw up their hands in the air, thinking that things will never change. At times like this, it can be helpful to shake things up a bit. Think about how different your living room can feel when you rearrange the furniture. It is the same sofa, in the same room, sitting on the same floor. But because you change the order of things, so follows your perception. Many situations do not require a complete "rearrangement of the furniture." Sometimes all that is needed is a subtle shift to make a world of difference. Below are a series of questions designed to help investigate some possible changes of scenery. Please fill out the questions below.

1. In the following paragraph, please provide an account of a typical example of the troubling pattern.

_____

_____

_____

_____

_____

_____

2. Being as specific as possible, where does this usually take place?

_____

_____

3. On what day or days of the week does this occur?

_____

_____

4. During what time or times during the day?

_____

_____

Below, space is provided for you to brainstorm ways in which to alter the circumstances surrounding specific episodes in the cycle. Because this is brainstorming, no answer or possibility should be discounted.

1. Instead of the current location, where could current instances such as that described above be moved?

_____

_____

_____

_____

2. What differing day of the week could contribute to an alteration of the cycle?

_____

_____

_____

_____

3. What change in time of day would help manage the situation?

_____

_____

_____

4. What strategies would be needed to accomplish any of these changes?

_____

_____

_____

_____

V.2   *Keeping the Momentum: Being Proactive and Enhancing Change*

Therapist's Overview

Purpose of the Exercise

Have you ever worked with a client or family who showed great progress in the first few sessions and wondered how to maintain that progress? Building early progress into systemic change is at the heart of SSB therapy. By overtly assessing client progress, you acknowledge and document change and increase the client's self-efficacy in their life. The focus of this exercise is on keeping client progress moving by building ongoing assessment throughout the counseling process.

Suggestions for Use

1. This exercise can be used as a tool to summarize client or family progress and as a means to determine future goals.
2. This exercise can be used with all individuals or families and may be most beneficial after the first few sessions as an ongoing assessment tool.
3. This exercise may also work well with individuals who are concrete analytic thinkers who would benefit from written documentation of their progress.
4. This exercise may also be modified to be used after each session as a case note that you write with your client or family. Weekly "report cards" may be an excellent means to track progress, plan future goals, and increase collaboration between you and your client.

Exercise

Perhaps the most optimal time to begin this exercise is when writing case notes and planning for the next session. This exercise will describe a way to summarize client progress and examine upcoming sessions from a new perspective.

The Narrative Report Card

When I write a narrative report card, I frame it as a letter of reference and describe the client's strengths and resources, point out specific exceptions to their complaints, and note how they have maintained changes. I also try to include a paragraph presupposing continued change. During our next session, I show my client the narrative report card, and we discuss the letter together. I believe it is a positive, concrete reminder of the client's hard work and a method to summarize and plan for future change.

1. Now that you have read your report card, what are your thoughts regarding your progress?

_____

_____

2. What was the most meaningful aspect of your report card?

_____

_____

3. What do you think is the next step now that you progressed this far?

_____

_____

4. If you were going to write your own report card, what would you write?

_____

_____

5. What will your report card look like in two weeks?

_____

_____

V.3   You Don't Say: The "No-Talk" Client

Therapist's Overview

Purpose of the Exercise

In talk therapies, it is often assumed that people must engage in conversation for change to occur. Although conversation makes therapy more interesting and typically presents more opportunities to promote change, some clients will choose to be less talkative or say nothing at all. This can be the case with some children, adolescents, or people who have felt unheard, felt unacknowledged, or had negative experiences in therapy in the past. From an SSB perspective, we do not view these persons as resistant, avoidant, unmotivated, or oppositional. Instead, we see these actions by clients as communication that they need something different from us. The purpose of this exercise is to engage clients in patterns that involve acknowledgement and permission to not speak and increase the benefits of each therapeutic interaction.

Suggestions for Use

1. This exercise can be used at any point in therapy.
2. The aim of this exercise is to interact with clients in ways that are likely to increase the potential benefits of therapy. It is not to make people talk.
3. We want to keep in mind that change is constant. Although a person may not engage in verbal conversation, he or she can still benefit from positive interactions.
4. Cross-reference: Perhaps first completing Exercise I.3, "Creating New Meaning: All Our Actions Are Meaningful," will make this exercise more effective.

Exercise

Sometimes people just do not want to talk. There are many reasons for this. Rather than delving into motivation or attempting to explain behavior, when people talk less or not at all we attend to it as communication. We also focus on other ways of encouraging change through acknowledgement, permission, and specific methods. This exercise is to help you as a practitioner to work with clients who may be less verbal. To complete this exercise, follow the suggestions below. Then write your own example in the spaces provided.

Points of Consideration

1. *Acknowledge and Normalize*—When people do not want to talk, we want to acknowledge this experience and let them know we understand and that other people have felt the same way. This also normalizes clients' experiences.

2. *Give Permission*—In addition to acknowledgement, it is important to extend permission by letting the client know it is "okay" to not talk. To do this we say, "If you don't feel like talking that's perfectly acceptable" or "It's okay if you don't feel like talking." It is not that clients need our permission; however, it lets them know that we respect them.

3. *Invite the Person to Talk in the Future*—It is also important to leave the door open to future conversation by inviting clients to talk at a later time, when they are ready. We can do this by saying, "I want you to know that if you decide down the road—perhaps later on in our meeting

today or sometime in a future meeting—that you would like to talk, I'll be here for you. I'll leave that up to you."

4. *Change the Pattern by Leading the Discussion or Taking the Lead*—Our aim is not to make people talk. Instead, we want to create opportunities for change. So, we bear in mind that people can change without talking. Instead of pushing for clients to talk, we can take care to avoid patterns that require clients to respond. One way to do this is to take the lead in conversations by using humor, self-disclosure, storytelling, and other ways of relating that do not require clients to speak.

5. *Combine Methods*—By combining the various elements described, we can create a context in which there is an increased likelihood that clients will feel acknowledged, which, in turn, increases the likelihood that they will be open to what follows. Here are two examples:

   a. It's okay if you don't feel like talking right now. I sometimes feel that way. Perhaps later you'll feel more up to it, but if not, that's okay too. Maybe we can use this time in a different way. Actually, I was thinking about how this reminds me of a friend of mine whom I consider to be very wise and open-minded. She does a lot of listening and uses her words sparingly. She observes a lot and then when she's ready, she talks, and not a minute before. I'm wondering to myself if that's the kind of person you are. Then again, it may be something different altogether for you.

   b. I want you to know that it's absolutely fine if you prefer not to say much today. I was thinking that today might be a really good day for you to take a break from talking. Actually, I've got a lot to say anyway, so I'm glad you're here. So if you don't mind I'd just like to share some things I've been thinking about. For example, the other night I was watching the news and I saw this story about this man who takes animals in and nurses them back to health then releases them to the wild. I think this really hit home with me not just because of his kindness, but because he has found something that he is passionate about.

These examples represent just the beginning of conversations that we could initiate with clients. These conversations should not be random. They should minimally acknowledge, validate, and invite. They should speak to clients' interests or concerns in ways that encourage rather than inhibit, blame, or close down possibilities. If a particular direction is not met with some client verbal engagement that does not mean the client is not benefiting. At the same time, it is up to the therapist to try different avenues if a particular tack does not work.

Taking the Lead

Now it is your turn. Incorporating the suggestions offered earlier, create your own conversational sequence you might initiate with a client who is less verbal.

_____

_____

_____

_____

_____

_____

_____

_____

_____

_____

_____

_____

_____

V.4   Changing It Up: Altering Problem Patterns

Therapist's Overview

Purpose of the Exercise

Problems can seem to develop lives of their own, particularly when they become patterned. This is when problems repeat over and over. Sometimes it takes only a small change in one part of a pattern to get things going in a better direction. The idea is to first identify unhelpful patterns and then search for small areas where these patterns can be interrupted, altered, or changed in some way. The purpose of this exercise is to introduce some change in patterns as a means of breaking them up.

Suggestions for Use

1. It is generally a good idea to suggest that people concentrate on making small changes in patterns as opposed to trying to change everything at once.
2. Be sure that whatever clients intend to do differently is reasonable and achievable. This way it will not be hard to undertake and will not require major changes in the person's lifestyle. This will also lower the degree of difficulty for clients, and new changes are more likely to be employed on a regular or ongoing basis.
3. This exercise can be done with individuals, couples, or families. If more than one person is involved, have each person choose a way of changing the pattern and complete the exercise. Then compare each person's responses.

Exercise

Our lives are full of patterns. Many of these patterns help us to accomplish things and live our lives. Other times they interfere and are disruptive. The trouble is that we do not always notice when patterns have become problematic. The good news is that very often only small changes are necessary to change problem patterns. This exercise can help you to both identify and change patterns with yourself and in relationships. To complete this exercise, write your response to each inquiry in the spaces provided.

1. Describe a typical pattern that happens in your life that you would like to change. It could be a pattern that represents a habit or a way of interacting with others. Remember that a pattern is anything, positive or negative, that repeats itself. Patterns involve the actions of individuals and interactions between people. For example, a pattern might be that when you disagree with someone at work you withdraw and close down. This then makes you even more upset and you withdraw further. The result is you do not get your subsequent work done. This process then leads to further problems at work.

_____

_____

_____

_____

2. Next, pick a way to change the pattern in a way that might improve things just a bit. You will want to also commit to doing the new pattern at least three times in the next week. Write down what you plan to do. Remember to keep the change small and "doable."

_____

_____

_____

_____

3. After you try out your new pattern for a week, write down the three instances where you acted differently.

   a. _____

   b. _____

   c. _____

4. What difference did it make to change your actions involved in the pattern?

_____

_____

_____

_____

5. How did changing the pattern change the problem you were facing?

_____

_____

_____

_____

6. What does this tell you about yourself?

_____

_____

_____

_____

V.5   *Being a Creature of Habit: Identifying, Establishing, and Maintaining Rituals*

Therapist's Overview

Purpose of the Exercise

We often think of routines as habits. Some habits are more important than others as they connect people and bring out consistency in relationships. In this sense, habits can also be referred to as rituals and might include specific dinnertimes, certain meals on certain days, movie nights, and so on. These activities are essential to both individual and relational development and can take place daily, weekly, monthly, seasonally, and yearly. The purpose of this exercise is to help individuals, couples, and families to build or maintain continuity and connection by identifying and continuing old rituals or establishing new ones.

Suggestions for Use

1. This exercise can be used with individuals, couples, or families.
2. Encourage people to involve others in conversations about rituals. Although some members of a family, for example, may seem less interested, help clients to remain aware that rituals do not have to always have high entertainment value. Even though fun rituals may be more exciting, the overall aim is to increase continuity and connection.
3. Rituals can be ones that are already in place. They can be old rituals that were disrupted due to some change in the family but can be restarted. Or, they can be completely new ones.

Exercise

Think of a time when you felt connected to others. Now think of a time when you felt safe and secure. Do you see any similarities in these situations? When we think of these types of scenarios, we often recount rituals such as family events, hanging out with friends, celebrations, and so on. A common theme with these situations and events is the consistency and stability they have brought to our individual lives and to our family and close social relationships. We refer to these as rituals, and they can occur on a daily, weekly, monthly, seasonal, or yearly basis. This exercise is to help identify your current rituals or if you have experienced a lapse in old rituals, to establish new ones. To complete this exercise, write your responses to the questions in the spaces provided.

1. What are the current activities or events in place with you or your family? You may want to think of rituals as routine things that happen on a very regular basis that involve family and friends. Please list each one individually.

   a. _____

   b. _____

   c. _____

   d. _____

   e. _____

2. How does each of the rituals you listed bring some connection or consistency to your life or to your family life?

    a. _____

    b. _____

    c. _____

    d. _____

    e. _____

3. What are examples of rituals that you had in place but for one reason or another were stopped or interrupted?

    a. _____

    b. _____

    c. _____

4. Which of the rituals you listed in Question #3 would you consider starting up again?

    a. _____

    b. _____

    c. _____

5. What difference might it make if you were to restart an old ritual?

_____

_____

_____

6. Schedule a meeting with your family or friends. Invite them to talk about ways that you might become further connected through new activities that could be done on a regular or consistent basis. Please list those new rituals below.

    a. _____

    b. _____

    c. _____

    d. _____

    e. _____

7. Take one of the new rituals that was created and try it a few times. Then write the results of that experiment below.

_____

_____

_____

_____

Be sure to track those rituals that seem to provide consistency and stability and promote relational cohesion.

V.6   The Economy of Movement: When Smaller Changes Lead to Bigger Ones

Therapist's Overview

Purpose of the Exercise

One of the ways we can be agents of change is by helping the people with whom we work to notice small indicators of positive change and movement toward their goals. This means first noting the intensity of concerns and then identifying and amplifying moments that are in contrast to those concerns. This means observing for times, no matter how small, that concerns are less intrusive or dominating and when people are clear about what was different about those times. This can help to build momentum toward the future. The purpose of this exercise is help orient clients' attention toward differences in the duration and intensity of concerns, exploring the actions associated with these variations and changes. It is through smaller changes that bigger ones can evolve.

Suggestions for Use

1. This exercise can be used at any point in therapy.
2. This exercise can be completed in therapy or can be suggested as a task to complete outside of therapy. In either case, it is important to discuss the importance of noticing how small changes can lead to bigger ones and that sometimes positive change is a matter of "getting the ball rolling."

Exercise

Sometimes small changes ultimately lead to bigger ones. It is therefore important to keep an eye out for differences in both the duration and intensity of your concern as well as small positive movements and identifying factors that contributed to any changes in these areas. This exercise can assist you with focusing on changes that may have occurred in relation to the concerns you have been facing and how you can capitalize on these changes to achieve your goals. To complete this exercise, please write your responses in the spaces provided.

1. Consider the concern that you have been facing. If you have been challenged by several, for now, select the one that has been most pressing. When you are ready, take a moment to play through the biggest "flare-up" you had. That is, go to a recent time when the problem peaked in terms of its interference in your life. Play through the series of events surrounding the flare-up and then write down the sequence below.

_____

_____

_____

_____

2. Reflecting back on the sequence you wrote above, what do you think kept things from getting worse? What did you do?

_____

_____

_____

_____

3. Next, think about a time when the concern was present but it was not quite as intense as the way you described previously. What kept things from escalating further?

_____

_____

_____

_____

4. What did you learn about the concern you have been facing?

_____

_____

_____

_____

5. Let us now change gears. Over the next day or two, notice any differences, however small, that occur in the intensity of the concern. In the table provided, rate the concern in terms of its duration (how long it lasted) and its intensity (how intrusive or disruptive it was) on a scale from 1 to 10, with 1 meaning the concern was not intrusive at all and 10 meaning that the concern has been very overwhelming. For example, a 3 on the "How Long" scale might mean the problem only lasted for a few minutes, whereas an 8 might indicate that it was present for a longer, extended period.

Time of Day	"How Long" Rating	Intensity Rating
6:00 a.m.–7:00 a.m.		
7:00 a.m.–8:00 a.m.		
9:00 a.m.–10:00 a.m.		
10:00 a.m.–11:00 a.m.		
11:00 a.m.–12:00 p.m.		

Time of Day	"How Long" Rating	Intensity Rating
12:00 p.m.–1:00 p.m.		
1:00 p.m.–2:00 p.m.		
2:00 p.m.–3:00 p.m.		
3:00 p.m.–4:00 p.m.		
4:00 p.m.–5:00 p.m.		
5:00 p.m.–6:00 p.m.		
6:00 p.m.–7:00 p.m.		
7:00 p.m.–8:00 p.m.		
8:00 p.m.–9:00 p.m.		
9:00 p.m.–10:00 p.m.		
10:00 p.m.–11:00 p.m.		
11:00 p.m.–12:00 a.m.		
12:00 a.m.–1:00 a.m.		
1:00 a.m.–2:00 a.m.		
2:00 a.m.–3:00 a.m.		
3:00 a.m.–4:00 a.m.		
4:00 a.m.–5:00 a.m.		
5:00 a.m.–6:00 a.m.		

6. Looking over the past 24 hours, what did you notice about the duration and intensity of your concern?

_____

_____

_____

7. What was different about the times when the problem was at its lowest in terms of its level of interference in your life?

_____

_____

_____

8. What things, however small, did you do differently when your concern has been less dominating? Be specific.

_____

_____

_____

_____

9. What could you do differently with this information?

_____

_____

_____

_____

V.7   *Decision Making and a Healthy Amount of Worry: Making Stress Your Friend*

Therapist's Overview

Purpose of the Exercise

Conceivably the best predictor of coping with a new challenge is prechallenge coping ability. Knowing how one copes is an important component of knowing who a person is. Are you a planner, procrastinator, or fly-by-the-seat-of-your-pants person? The purpose of this exercise is for clients to better understand how they cope and ultimately make decisions.

Decision making and coping strategies go hand in hand. Often poor coping leads to poor decisions and beneficial coping leads to proactive decision making. However, the question remains, how do we increase positive coping and decision making? Perhaps anxiety is the answer. When individuals have a healthy amount of anxiety they take the time to cope with their issues and make a sound decision. When there is not enough anxiety, individuals do not take their concern seriously enough and faulty decisions arise. Moreover, when anxiety reaches unproductive levels, individuals lose some ability to sort through options to make a sound decision.

Suggestions for Use

1. This exercise can be beneficial with clients who are having difficulty making decisions.
2. This exercise may also be beneficial if you are concerned with demystifying the counseling process by explain coping and decision making.
3. This exercise can also be utilized when discussing with clients how to sustain change.

Exercise

To begin this exercise, ask your client to remember and describe a time when the client felt he or she coped with a stressful situation. A second question to ask your client to start this exercise is to think about a time when the client made a good decision. Here are some additional follow-up questions to highlight their first answers.

1. How do you know you are coping and making good decisions?

_____

_____

2. What needs to happen for you to cope well and make good decisions?

_____

_____

3. In what ways can you take your ability to make decisions and cope and translate it to your current situation?

_____

_____

4. What is going on around you that lets you know you are on the right path?

_____

_____

5. When things are getting just a little bit worse, what do you do to prevent them from getting totally out of control?

_____

_____

6. How would you describe your actions in a stress-free environment?

_____

_____

7. How would you describe your actions in a high-stress environment?

_____

_____

8. What needs to happen for you to keep your stress at a manageable level?

_____

_____

9. If you were to teach someone how to make good decisions, what would you do?

_____

_____

V.8   *From Mountains to Molehills: Taking Things One Step at a Time*

Therapist's Overview

Purpose of the Exercise

Most struggles are not accompanied by a single, discreet impact. Dealing with a flat tire is troublesome, plus it may also result in tardiness for an appointment, lack of cell phone connection, spoiled groceries, a headache, or crying children. So, too, does this characterize the struggles of many of our clients. This exercise is intended to dissect all the various components and consequences of a single concern. Next, it will help focus energy on that which is tangible and doable. They will be encouraged to identify more incremental activities that may nonetheless lead to more dramatic change.

Suggestions for Use

1. This exercise is intended for use with clients who express overwhelming concern over a particular challenge.
2. It is appropriate for all ages and can be used in family sessions with minimal modification.
3. Cross-reference: This exercise can be augmented when used with exercise II.7, "What Does That Look Like? Translating Ambiguity Through Action-Talk."

Exercise

All of us face challenges at times that seem overwhelming and, like a mountain, impossible to climb. Rather than attempting to scale the mountain all at once, it is useful and sometimes less daunting to list all of the challenges that may be faced on the way to the summit. The known is typically less scary than the unknown, after all.

1. Below, please write down your primary concern today (i.e., loss of a job, tension in a relationship, academic struggles, etc.).

_____

_____

2. Next, please make a list of all of the challenges that go with your primary concern (inability to pay bills, loneliness, loss of privileges, etc.).

_____

_____

3. Looking over your list, which two items do you have the most control or influence over?

_____

_____

4. Which of these two items is more concerning to you right now?

_____

_____

5. What are one or two things you could do to address this problem?

_____

_____

6. How feasible are these options?

_____

_____

7. When you address this, how would that impact the larger concern?

_____

_____

V.9   Raindrops on Roses and Whiskers on Kittens: What Are My Favorite Things?

Therapist's Overview

Purpose of the Exercise

An effective therapist will constantly emphasize the client's growth and change. To some, though, "change" is a daunting concept that seems too grandiose to be realized. The purpose of this exercise is to help the client build on his or her current preferences to help the change process build greater momentum. Its emphasis is on practical, manageable activity that can provide the client with swift successes from which the client can move toward broader long-term goals.

Suggestions for Use

1. This exercise can be used toward the beginning of the therapeutic process to provide tangible movement toward goals and relief of presenting concerns.
2. The lists generated can be revised at any time to continue to reflect change and progress.
3. Cross-reference: This exercise can be used as an additive to Exercise II.11, "Future Screening: Creating a Vision for the Future."

Exercise

When people state they wish to make a change in their lives, they sometimes do not know where to begin. Changes in vocation, social circles, family relationships, and individual perception are common goals that can feel initially too great to be achieved. It is important to remember that change comes in all shapes and sizes and should be characterized by what you already know and enjoy. This activity is intended to help you highlight your favorite things and to assist you in brainstorming how to add to or alter them in some way to provide you with new experiences and learning.

1. Please list your favorite activities.

_____

_____

_____

_____

_____

_____

_____

_____

2. On a scale of 1 to 10, with 10 being the highest, which activity would you rate the highest?

_____

Rating: _____

3. What do you think and feel while doing this activity?

_____

_____

4. How could you do this activity in a way you have never tried before?

_____

_____

5. If done in this new way, how would you rate this activity?

_____

_____

6. What obstacles could keep you from trying the new form of the activity?

_____

_____

7. What could be done to remove these obstacles?

_____

_____

8. How long will it take to make this new version of the activity possible?

_____

_____

9. How would your life be different if you completed this new form of your favorite activity?

_____

_____

V.10   *Replacing Street Behavior: Walking the Fine Line*

Therapist's Overview

Purpose of the Exercise

If a central feature of strengths and solution-based (SSB) therapy is meeting clients "where they are at" and embracing their experiences and worldview; how can this be accomplished effectively when clients have beliefs and norms that were once self-protective but now are less protective and more detrimental? A number of individuals who were reentering society from prison have discussed coping strategies that resembled an eye for an eye or worse. In the past, for these individuals, if they were not overly defensive and combative, it probably would have meant great harm or even death. The question remains, how can we respect our clients' experience and also provide ethical and effective services?

The purpose of this exercise is to collaborate with your client on developing appropriate coping mechanisms for the client's new environments in which he or she lives. More specifically, how can clients replace unhealthy norms and values with more pro-social values to better operate and interact in society?

Suggestions for Use

1. This exercise could be beneficial to adolescents who are transitioning their coping strategies from ones of confrontation to collaboration and compromise.
2. This exercise may also be beneficial to individuals who are transitioning from environments where it was advantageous to be hyperindividualistic (i.e., prison, living on the street) to environments where the norm is more communal than individualistic.

Exercise

A beneficial starting place to begin this exercise is to examine your personal values and how you see the world. If you have not done so already, review or complete the exercises in Section I to ensure you have a sound understanding of your counseling ability. Having a personal awareness of your counseling ability and values may provide greater insight into separating your values from those of your clients and thus have a better chance for success.

The following questions may help the client recognize and implement new coping mechanisms.

1. When you examine your past stressful situations and how you handled them, what positives come to mind?

_____

_____

2. As you think about those situations further, what specific role did you play in the positive outcomes?

_____

_____

3. How is (insert client's poor coping mechanism) helpful in this situation?

_____

_____

4. When you think back to stressful situations and outcomes that were not positive, what role did your coping or actions play in the outcome?

_____

_____

5. What aspects of your coping are you willing to change?

_____

_____

6. When you think about your future work or relationships, how can you change just a little bit to stay employed or enhance your relationships?

_____

_____

7. What values do you hold close to your heart, and how do they interact with your decision making?

_____

_____

8. How can you make a decision that may be against your values and still save face?

_____

_____

A further suggestion to think about: Have your clients write their own revised life story to assess progress and set future goals.

V.11   *Taking Stock: Clients Increasing Their Control Over Their Lives*

Therapist's Overview

Purpose of the Exercise

Conceivably, when clients are in the process of "taking stock" of their progress, they are in a pivotal stage of their counseling. From a counseling perspective, a strong therapeutic relationship is present and clients are "living" with their changes and possibly heading into an area of their lives where they have never been or have not been in a long time. For many of my clients, this is the point where they express concern for taking more control of their life and at the same time are anxious about the uncertainty that living with change produces. For example, many clients know that they have to change and work hard to change but are equally scared of failing at their new life (i.e., "What if I am no good at being clean, a good parent, or a student"). The purpose of this exercise is to instill hope in your clients' progress and establish means for them to succeed in their future change and to take more control of their lives.

Suggestions for Use

1. This exercise can be beneficial with older adolescents, adults, and families when they have begun the change process and are progressing toward meeting their goals.
2. This exercise can be used as a means to assess client progress, as a method to summarize past sessions and set future goals.

Exercise

An ideal way to begin this exercise is when writing case notes and or planning future sessions. In essence, you and your client are both "taking stock" in the counseling process. Assess when your client has begun and met a few goals toward change. At this point, your client may be coming to a transition point in his or her life and an extra emphasis on instilling hope and internal control of the client's life may provide the needed reassurance to sustain change. Below are a few questions that can help your client assess his or her progress, identify possible trouble spots, and maintain change.

1. Looking back over the success you have had in making change, what are you most proud of?

_____

_____

2. Describe the role you played in creating and maintaining change.

_____

_____

3. In looking ahead to your continued success, what can you take from this experience that will help in sustaining change?

_____

_____

4. Now that you are more aware of your strengths and areas of improvement, name one or two things that you can do to stay focused and increase the control you have in your life.

_____

_____

5. If you were to encounter a trouble spot in the near future, what do you think would be the first sign that you are headed for trouble?

_____

_____

6. If you were to counsel yourself regarding this trouble spot, what would be the first question you ask to ease your difficulty?

_____

_____

7. If you were to describe an ideal person or someone you look up to, what qualities do they have that would help you maintain your success?

_____

Here is a further suggestion to think about: As a method to model for your client to have increased control of his or her life, you can allow more input during your client's session. If you have not done so already, have your client determine the duration of the session, focus, homework assignments, and so forth. Your role truly becomes one of facilitator and sounding board.

V.12   Shuffling the Deck: Creating Cards to Create Change

Therapist's Overview

Purpose of the Exercise

Therapists should not be afraid to introduce an element of fun into clinical sessions. Games can be an effective way to demystify the process and produce a change in perception. The purpose of this exercise is to offer a structured way for clients to investigate alterations in daily habits and ingrained patterns that may be taken for granted. Clients should be encouraged to keep an open mind so that even seemingly slight changes in pattern can be examined for potential benefit.

Suggestions for Use

1. This exercise may be helpful for clients who find themselves in static routines but who have difficulty identifying specific paths of change.
2. This can be used for individuals, couples, and families.
3. It is necessary to have index cards and pens available for this exercise.
4. This exercise can be used as an additive to Exercise V.8, "From Mountains to Mole Hills: Taking Things One Step at a Time."

Exercise

Everyone has their routines. Almost without thinking, most of us go through our days and weeks getting up at around the same time, spending our time in familiar ways, and engaging in similar activities. This activity is intended to help you take a look at some of your habits and patterns in a way that may allow you to see them in a different way. To complete it, please take 12 index cards. Now divide those cards into four groups of three. On one card in each group, write a different day of the week. Next, on the second card of each group, write an activity in which you participate on that day. On the third card in the groups, write the usual length of time you engage in that activity. An example of the groups can be seen below.

- **Card 1 (Group 1)**
  Day: Saturday

- **Card 2 (Group 1)**
  Activity: Jogging

- **Card 3**
  Time: 30 Minutes

Now that you have all of your cards, combine and shuffle the day cards as a group, then the activity cards, and finally the time cards. After shuffling, draw a card from each category and combine to form a new combination. Continue to draw as many times as desired.

Finally, ask yourself the following questions:

1. How would the activity be different if you chose to do it on this particular day?

_____

_____

_____

2. Are there any other exercises you would like to do on this day?

_____

_____

_____

3. Are there any barriers on this day that prevent this activity from happening? Do the barriers change if the time is altered to reflect your draw?

_____

_____

_____

4. Can you think of a different way in which you would like to use the time you drew?

_____

_____

_____

5. How would the activity change if you chose to participate in it for this period of time?

_____

_____

_____

SECTION VI

NARRATIVES OF TRANSFORMATION
Change, Progress, Transitions, and Endings

VI.1   *Building Momentum: Extending Change Into the Future*

Therapist's Overview

Purpose of the Exercise

We are continuously working with clients to monitor for change and to help them determine the relationship between those changes and overall goals. This translates to both identifying and amplifying change. By identifying change, we mean we help clients to notice what specifically has been better. Amplifying change relates to how the change came about. The purpose of this exercise is to help clients build on changes that they made in the direction of their goals. This can create momentum toward futures that are reflective of the kinds of lives clients want for themselves.

Suggestions for Use

1. This exercise can be used with individuals, couples, or families.
2. This exercise can be used for people in or out of therapy. If the person using this exercise is not in therapy, he or she can focus on what changes from week to week, for example, as opposed to session to session.
3. Even when positive change has happened, because clients may be experiencing other problems or have other things on their minds, they often do not immediately notice those changes. It is therefore important to remain change focused and exercise patience. Continue to focus on small changes.

Exercise

Although change is constant, we do not always notice that it is happening. If we focus our attention on change, however, we often notice that problems are less dominating or disruptive and that progress is occurring in relation to overall goals. In fact, sometimes the change that has already taken place is sufficient enough to determine that goals have been met. This exercise will help you to identify positive changes that occurred with your concern and the degree to which your goal has been met. You can then work to build upon these changes for the future. To complete this exercise, write your responses to the questions in the spaces provided.

1. What is the smallest thing you noticed that has changed for the better with the problem you have been facing? Be as specific as possible, listing each behavior, action, or interaction by using clear, action-based descriptions.

_____

_____

_____

_____

_____

2. When did you first notice that things had changed? What did you notice happening at that time? Be as specific as possible, listing each behavior, action, or interaction by using clear, action-based descriptions.

_____

_____

_____

_____

_____

3. How did the change happen? What did you do? What did members of your family do? Be as specific as possible, listing each behavior, action, or interaction by using clear, action-based descriptions.

_____

_____

_____

_____

_____

4. How did you get yourself to do what you did?

_____

_____

_____

_____

5. How was what you did different than what you have done in the past?

_____

_____

_____

_____

6. How has the change been helpful to you?

_____

_____

_____

_____

_____

7. What will be different in the future as these changes continue?

_____

_____

_____

_____

_____

8. Who else noticed the changes you described?

_____

_____

_____

_____

_____

9. How might that person or persons benefit from these changes?

_____

_____

_____

_____

_____

10. How does the change you experienced relate to the overall goals you set for yourself (or with your relationship or family)? How much closer are you to reaching those goals? What might be a next step for you?

_____

_____

_____

_____

_____

VI.2 Developing Your Own Take-Home Message: Tell Me What You Think

Therapist's Overview

Purpose of the Exercise

Perhaps one of the greatest factors in counseling is the client's motivation or readiness for change. Collaborating with your clients on their goals and on their focus for counseling will go a long way in establishing a strong therapeutic relationship. The purpose of this exercise is to work with your clients on developing their recognition in their ability to change.

One way to accomplish this is by discussing decision making and the change process. Another way to assess and increase client readiness is to ask clients to write or vocalize their take-home message for the counseling session. A "take-home message" is simply what your client thought was most meaningful about his or her session. In this form, the take-home message is a very basic outcome rating and a means to overtly "know" from your client's perspective the usefulness of the session.

Suggestions for Use

1. This exercise is written for clients at any point of counseling.
2. This exercise could be used as a summary statement.
3. This exercise could be used to transition from one topic to another and also to begin the discussion of termination.
4. Cross-reference: See Exercise VI.6, "Giving Credit to Yourself: A New Look In the Mirror."

Exercise

We all have the ability to change, and yet there are times when we lose confidence and doubt ourselves. This exercise can help you to rebuild that confidence in your ability to influence your situation and your life and to be an active participant in change. To complete this exercise, have your therapist (or on your own) walk you through the phases listed below.

1. To start this exercise, ask your client, with at least 15 minutes left, what was most meaningful. Another way you can frame this question is to ask your client, "When you are on your way home, what will be the one or two things that stand out as most important?"

Client's Response

_____

_____

_____

_____

_____

_____

2. After hearing your client's response, discuss with him or her any affective, cognitive, and behavioral components of his or her message. By doing so, your client will be better able to acknowledge change and continue the change process.

Here are additional examples for developing a take-home message.

1. When you are transitioning from one topic to another, you could ask your client, "Before we completely change our focus, I'd like to ask, what resonates most with you?"

2. When beginning the transition to completing counseling, you could ask your client, "When you envision that you no longer need to come to counseling, what will be your take-home message to yourself?"

This is another suggestion to think about: A way to further utilize a take-home message is to have both you and your client develop a message and then share your message and give rationale for your choice.

VI.3   *Filling the Void: It Can Be Better Than You Thought*

Therapist's Overview

Purpose of the Exercise

A central aspect of strengths and solution-based (SSB) therapy is going beyond symptom removal and working with clients on filling the void that was their complaint. For example, the change process is more than stopping substance abuse; it is recognizing individual strengths to utilize instead of a substance during times of stress. Sustained change is going beyond miracle thinking (all I need to do is this one thing and all will be better) and increasing individual strengths and positive coping mechanisms.

The purpose of this exercise is to have clients develop positive coping mechanisms and an awareness of resources to help increase change. Moreover, this exercise will allow clients to recognize the "realities" of their life (i.e., just because they no longer use and abuse, it does not mean that their life is carefree). Clients' ability to have a realistic view of their lives will go a long way in positively filling their void.

Suggestions for Use

1. This exercise can work well when clients have begun the change process.
2. After a discussion of this exercise, it can be used as a gauge to know when to end counseling—when your client has filled his or her void.
3. Older adolescents and adults are well suited for this exercise.
4. This exercise can go well with all goal-setting exercises, and specifically, Exercise VI.6, "Giving Credit to Yourself: A New Look in the Mirror" and Exercise VI.2, "Developing Your Own Take-Home Message: Tell Me What You Think."

Exercise

To begin this exercise, have your client describe the progress he or she has made toward his or her goals. During this discussion, focus on resources and appropriate coping mechanisms of your client as well as miracle thinking that he or she needs to be reframed to concentrate on realistic and obtainable goals. Below are some suggested follow-up questions you can use with your client to facilitate a positive filling of the void.

1. How will your life look once your complaint is no longer the main focus of your life?

_____

_____

_____

2. In order for you to sustain the change you made, what supports do you need?

_____

_____

_____

3. What words would you use to describe yourself after you changed your complaint?

_____

_____

_____

_____

4. What words would others use to describe you after you changed your complaint?

_____

_____

_____

_____

5. If you feel your complaint growing even a slight bit, what support will you use to decrease your complaint?

_____

_____

_____

_____

VI.4   Creating Your Own GPS: A New Map for a New Day

Therapist's Overview

Purpose of the Exercise

As the beginning chapters clearly illustrate, the importance of establishing client strengths, goals, and therapeutic relationships is paramount in competent and effective counseling, regardless of orientation or philosophy. However, equally important, but many times less emphasized, is a focus on evaluating change and planning for continued success. At the heart of this exercise are the core principles of SSB therapies. The use of questions allows clients to recognize resources and exceptions, set and meet goals, and work toward lasting change. Simply, how can the client utilize personal resources and past success to induce change in the present and future and thus create a new vision of the self?

Perhaps a useful way to conceptualize this exercise is to have your client think about his or her change as a map and the client's self as a GPS—a unique internal device that remembers past directions and has access to new locations. Simply, creating your own GPS is an internal system that will not allow individuals to get lost. A personal GPS will allow individuals to venture out and take new roads while not forgetting the tried and true maneuvers of success. The end result of this exercise should allow the client to acknowledge and value past success, assess where the client is at meeting his or her goals, and create a plan for continued progress.

Suggestions for Use

1. This exercise could work well with individuals who are planners or structured individuals.
2. This exercise could also work well with individuals who are having difficulty visualizing and embracing the change they made.
3. Counselors who believe they are skilled at reframing could be well skilled with this exercise.
4. This exercise can be easily modified and shortened to be used at the beginning of every session.
5. This exercise would work well in conjunction with any of the exercises in this section.

Exercise

To begin this exercise most effectively, utilize it at a point during a session when you are looking to summarize or illustrate the past and point out future progress. The following are some questions that will help in this process.

1. When you reflect back on the past few weeks, what are you most proud of accomplishing?

_____

_____

2. What parts of yourself allowed you to plan, implement, and sustain the changes you made?

_____

_____

3. Have you noticed the changes becoming easier to make in your life?

_____

_____

4. How can you utilize what you have learned here in the future as a map for continued progress?

_____

_____

5. If you experience another complaint, how can you use this current experience to gain your bearings to find your direction?

_____

_____

6. How do you think you can make your GPS more effective?

_____

_____

7. If someone asked you for your thoughts on creating his or her own GPS, what words of wisdom would you have?

_____

_____

VI.5 *Building the Fire Inside: Sustaining Change in Your Life*

Therapist's Overview

Purpose of the Exercise

This exercise uses a metaphor of building a fire to help your client describe his or her stage of change. Moreover, this exercise emphasizes ways to stabilize, sustain, and grow client progress. Similar to the "miracle" question, this exercise asks your client to look at his or her complaint differently to envision a new reality that the client can create and live.

The intent of this metaphoric exercise is to have individuals examine their lives from a slightly different perspective, thus allowing for new possibilities of change to enter into their consciousness to start or continue their change process. The strength in this exercise comes from building on the idea of your clients' desire and motivation for change as a passionate fire burning inside of them—their fuel needed to complete the change process.

Suggestions for Use

1. This exercise may be helpful with clients with whom you have a therapeutic relationship established.
2. This exercise is helpful when working with individuals on building individual hope.
3. This exercise may be used when the change process has occurred and the client is looking to sustain change.
4. This exercise could also be helpful to individuals who are visual and enjoy the outdoors.

Exercise

To begin this exercise, ask your clients to visualize their motivation for change as a fire burning inside their bodies. Similar to scaling questions, their description of their personal fire will direct your subsequent questions. For example, if your client responds that their fire is out, they are early on in their readiness for change. If their fire is burning bright and hot, their change is well under way. Below are additional questions that could be utilized with this exercise.

Questions to ask with clients early on in the change process:

1. How would you go about collecting the necessary tinder to start your fire?

_____

_____

_____

_____

_____

2. Who would be the person you turn to help you in collecting your tinder?

_____

_____

_____

3. What would be the one thing needed to generate a spark to start your fire?

_____

_____

Questions to ask when your client is a little farther along in his or her change process:

1. Now that your fire is burning, what needs to happen to keep it burning?

_____

_____

_____

2. What can you do to not only keep your fire burning, but also to make it burn brighter and hotter?

_____

_____

_____

3. If you see rain in the forecast, what can you do to protect your fire from going out?

_____

_____

_____

4. How can you stockpile your wood supply so that you have wood when you most need it?

_____

_____

_____

VI.6 *Giving Credit to Yourself: A New Look in the Mirror*

Therapist's Overview

Purpose of the Exercise

One of the central features of SSB therapy is changing personal perception of negativity to a belief in personal assets and strengths. The purpose of this exercise is to work with your clients in changing their view of their selves. I have found that most clients can easily blame themselves for their shortcomings while at the same time have real difficulties giving themselves praise or credit for the changes they made and are making.

One way to start the change process is for individuals to put an end to blaming themselves for their past behaviors and invest their energy into personal strengths and recognize individual control in the change process. This change in focus will allow your clients to start and view themselves from a different perspective and "recreate" their new realities—a reality of possibility and strength.

Suggestions for Use

1. This exercise may be used with clients who are determining their goals.
2. This exercise may be helpful with clients who may be experiencing a slight regression in their change process.
3. This exercise can also be used as a way to establish client compliments.
4. This exercise may also work well if you tie it in with goal development exercises.
5. This exercise can also be used as a compliment exercise where the counselor acknowledges change—in writing, verbally, and even in a certificate.

Exercise

This exercise is to help you to take a new look at yourself. Sometimes when we glance at ourselves we see only certain things and miss others; but there is always so much more. It is a matter of taking a second look and noticing the unnoticed or the overlooked aspects of ourselves and our lives. To complete this exercise, write your responses to prompts in the spaces provided.

1. Think of something in your life that you are proud of.

_____

_____

2. Describe the role you had in that event.

_____

_____

3. Describe the emotion you experienced during the event.

_____

_____

Ask the above questions a number of times to have your client further acknowledge his or her ability to change and the client's role in the process. Next, work with your clients to transfer those positive experiences of them to what they are currently experiencing.

1. In what ways are your past successes similar to your current situation?

_____

_____

2. How can you take control of your current situation and create even a small amount of change?

_____

_____

3. Now that you started to make changes, how have you begun to see yourself differently?

_____

_____

VI.7   The Crossroads of Change: Maintaining New Patterns

Therapist's Overview

Purpose of the Exercise

This exercise can also be used in conjunction with Exercise VI.4, "Creating Your Own GPS: A New Map for a New Day." The intent of this exercise is for the client to increase his or her self-awareness to enhance positive, lasting change.

It is important for the client to increase his or her self-awareness in all areas of the client's life. This ability will only enhance the client's resiliency and adaptability to change. A significant portion of change is knowing how to deal with similar and new challenges that may arise. Having a plan to address the challenge or issue before it becomes disastrous will go a long way to creating positive, lasting change.

Suggestions for Use

1. This exercise could be beneficial as a tool for clients to use to gauge their progress and as a plan for future sessions.
2. An outcome of this exercise could be a good assessment of the counseling process and an idea when counseling is no longer needed for the client.

Exercise

A successful beginning to this exercise could be during the review with your client on the progress he or she has made.

1. How will you know old patterns of unproductive thinking or behavior are increasing?

_____

_____

2. What do you have to do to keep those thoughts or behaviors at a minimum?

_____

_____

3. When you are effectively dealing with your complaint, what thoughts, behaviors, and emotions are present?

_____

_____

4. When will you know you no longer have to come to counseling?

_____

_____

5. What needs to happen to make your last two sessions most productive?

_____

_____

6. How have you assessed the positive changes in your life?

_____

_____

7. What part of counseling was most important to you?

_____

_____

8. How will you reproduce successful aspects of counseling in other areas of your life?

_____

_____

VI.8 *In Honor of You: Incorporating Ritual Into the Transition Process*

Therapist's Overview

Purpose of the Exercise

In many cultures, rituals are utilized as powerful tools to mark a person's passage from one stage of life to another. They can be found on every continent from birth to death and at every point in between. Rituals are frequently celebrations of the successes that have come before and hopeful glances toward what comes next. By definition, a person in transition is in some degree in the process of significant change. And change can be difficult. This exercise is intended to incorporate the basic tenets of SSB therapy with ritual in order to lend further weight to the accomplishments of the client, consolidate therapeutic gains, and encourage hopeful anticipation for the future.

Suggestions for Use

1. Members of some cultures are less familiar and comfortable with the idea of ritual than others. Therefore, this exercise should be described in detail in advance of its utilization.
2. Some clients may want to invite friends and family members into the activity who are not normally involved in the therapeutic process. If so, it may be helpful to explain the scenario to the invitees.
3. It is helpful when planning this ritual to discuss with the client what he or she hopes to achieve at the conclusion of the ritual.
4. This exercise can be a powerful use of a termination or transition session and can be used during any significant change in a client's life.

Exercise

When moving from one significant period of life to another, many people find it important to mark the occasion. You worked diligently both in therapy and in the rest of your life to attain the goals you established for yourself. This activity is intended to honor and celebrate your work and to help prepare you for a bright future.

Part I: Homework

Between now and the next time we meet, please collect the following items and note the items and their significance in the spaces provided.

1. An item representing you at the beginning of therapy.

_____

_____

_____

2. An item representing you at some point in the future.

_____

_____

_____

3. A gift of thanks to yourself in honor of your achievement.

_____

_____

_____

4. A candle of your favorite color.

_____

_____

_____

5. An item representing how you will face future challenges.

_____

_____

_____

6. A list of the names of those who can help you in the future.

_____

_____

_____

7. Any other items you wish to include.

_____

_____

_____

Part II: Activity

Before the client arrives for the activity, the therapist will need to clear a shelf or table where the collected items can be placed.

When the client arrives and indicates he or she is ready, ask the client to take each item and place it on the prepared space. As each item is set down, invite the client to say aloud what the item is and what its significance is. The client should be encouraged to take as much time as needed. When all items are placed, ask the client if there is anything further he or she would like to say about the individual items or about the collection as a whole. This process should not be rushed. Allow time to process with the client any thoughts or feelings that may have arisen and if any aspect of the process proved to be surprising. Finally, ask the client if there is anything more that he or she needs to make the ritual complete.

VI.9   *Sharing the Credit: Acknowledging the Contributions of Others*

Therapist's Overview

Purpose of the Exercise

When positive change occurs, it can be particularly helpful to share credit for that change with others who were involved or who were supportive along the way. Sharing the credit involves focusing on relationships and acknowledging each person's contribution to improving overall situations. This can contribute to increased participation as clients who are left out of therapy processes can appear as noncompliant, resistant, and so unmotivated. In addition, it can serve as a countermeasure in situations where positive change has occurred and is being negated in some way. This is when clients make statements such as, "It will never last," "He's done that before," or "You haven't seen the real _____ yet." These comments often arise from clients who do not feel as if they made a valued or positive contribution to change. The purpose of this exercise is for therapists to engage clients in conversations where the credit for change is shared.

Suggestions for Use

1. This exercise is for therapists to use in therapy.
2. This exercise is best used with clients in couples or family therapy.
3. This exercise can be used at any point at which positive change occurred. It is important that therapists scan for any form of change, however small.

Exercise

When positive change occurs during therapy, it is common for those other than the "identified" clients to nullify or negate the change. This may not be intentional; however, it can have an unwanted effect on therapy. Consider, for example, what a person, such as a parent, might experience in a situation where change has happened quickly in therapy. Although problem resolution is the goal, it can also raise feelings of blame ("I'm a bad parent," "I clearly did a bad job") or inadequacy ("I obviously don't know what I'm doing," "Anyone could do a better job than me"). It may appear to a member of a couple or family that therapy was the reason change occurred and that their efforts over the years or course of a relationship were futile. Some clients will experience feelings of being a failure for not being able to fix problems and then invalidation when a stranger is able to "fix" the situation. In addition to invalidation, these effects can undermine therapy. The irony is that although others, such as family members, are often pointed to as the cause of problems, they do not always get credit for their individual contributions when things get better. This exercise is to identify the contributions of all those who may be involved, thus countering negative statements that can minimize change and prove invalidating. We refer to this as sharing the credit for change. To complete this exercise, please draw on the list of questions offered below and write your responses to any questions in the spaces provided.

Identify a situation in therapy in which positive change occurred with a couple or family (there is more than one person involved with therapy).

_____

_____

Next, draw on the following list of statements during your next session.

1. I wonder how you were able to instill the value of _____ in _____.

2. Like you, _____ seems to hold the value of _____ . I can't help thinking that he or she learned it from you.

3. It seems to me that _____ has learned the value of _____ from you.

4. What happened?

_____

_____

_____

5. How did your clients respond?

_____

_____

_____

_____

Next, draw on the following questions to evoke from clients something that they feel contributed to the change process. Again, try this out in a session.

1. How do you think your _____ (relationship, parenting, etc.) has contributed to _____'s ability to _____?

2. In what ways do you think you have been able to help _____ to stand up to adversity?

3. In what ways do you think you were of assistance in helping _____ to stand up to _____ and get back on track?

4. What happened?

_____

_____

_____

5. How did your clients respond?

_____

_____

_____

_____

_____

Finally, in a session, ask the primary client what contributions others made to his or her life, and then ask him or her to share those with others who are involved.

1. What did you learn from _____ about how to overcome _____?

2. Who taught you the value of _____?

3. From whom did you learn about _____?

4. What happened?

_____

_____

_____

_____

_____

5. How did your clients respond?

_____

_____

_____

_____

_____

Develop a list of a few questions you use in therapy to help share credit with others.

    1. _____

    2. _____

    3. _____

    4. _____

    5. _____

VI.10   *Maintaining the Course: Negotiating Future Hurdles*

Therapist's Overview

Purpose of Exercise

One of the challenges people face is maintaining the changes they made. Sometimes achieving change is easier than holding course once the change occurred. With a little thinking about the future, many of the potential hurdles people might face can be identified, which can neutralize threats to staying on course. The purpose of this exercise is to identify possible future hurdles to maintaining change and how clients can use their knowledge, skills, and "muscles of resilience" as they move into the future.

Suggestions for Use

1. This exercise can be used with individuals, couples, and families.
2. This exercise can be used at any point at which positive change has occurred. It can be especially useful at the end of therapy as a means of prevention.

Exercise

Achieving change is one thing. Maintaining it is another. The good news is that with a little forward thinking and anticipation, many potential future obstacles can be identified ahead of time and dealt with accordingly. In fact, you may even find that by thinking more about the future you will be more prepared for other concerns that might arise. This exercise is to help you to prepare for the future by thinking about possible hurdles and how you deal with them differently than in the past. To do this, you will use your abilities and resources and "muscles of resilience." To complete this exercise, please answer the questions offered and write your responses to any questions in the spaces provided.

For this first part, consider any possible hurdles you might face in maintaining the changes you made. Identifying possible hurdles does not mean that they will happen, only that you are considering things that potentially could get you off track.

1. What might be an indication to you that the problem was attempting to resurface? What might be the first sign?

_____

_____

_____

_____

_____

2. What will you do differently in the future if faced with the same or a similar problem?

_____

_____

_____

_____

_____

3. How can what you learned be of help to you in solving future problems?

_____

_____

_____

_____

_____

4. If you feel yourself slipping, what is one thing that can stop that slipping and get you back heading the direction you prefer?

_____

_____

_____

_____

_____

Now consider how you can not only maintain the gains you have made but extend them into the future.

1. How can you put your new understandings to work in the future?

_____

_____

_____

_____

2. What have you been doing that you will continue to do once therapy has ended and in the future?

_____

_____

_____

_____

_____

3. How will you continue to solidify and build on the changes that you made?

_____

_____

_____

_____

_____

4. After you leave here, what will you do to keep things going in the direction you prefer?

_____

_____

_____

_____

_____

5. How will you make sure that you will do that?

_____

_____

_____

_____

_____

6. How can you use what you learned in the future should you face a return of the same concern or something similar?

_____

_____

_____

_____

_____

Consider keeping your responses nearby as a reminder of your resilience and ability to manage change and adversity.

VI.11   Coming Soon to a Theater Near You: Preparing Clients for Their Next Great Adventure

Therapist's Overview

Purpose of the Exercise

Many clients find meaningful the experience of representing their growth in therapy in a tangible and visual way. This transition exercise can not only give representation to developed skills and insights, it can also elicit additional gains not immediately identified by the client. In addition, it can assist the client in developing a vision of how he or she hopes to build on successes in the near and far term. Most clients can relate to the posters in movie theaters that advertise films coming soon. The culmination of this exercise can result in a poster that reminds the client of his or her current achievements, and serves as a powerful hint of the great adventures to come.

Suggestions for Use

1. This exercise may proceed over the course of several sessions, so it should be initiated toward the beginning of the transition or termination process.
2. Families and couples may utilize this exercise to codify a more cohesive vision of the present and the future.
3. This exercise can be modified in any way that is more interesting to the client. The client can create an album cover, book jacket, or anything else that includes a future focus.
4. Cross-references: This exercise can be used as a bookend exercise with Exercise I.13, "Becoming the Hero of Your Own Story: Changing Narratives and Lives Through a Creative Process."

Exercise

Before the client's arrival, the therapist will need to assemble a variety of art materials. Some suggestions for supplies include the following:

• Construction paper	• String
• Magic Markers	• Glitter
• Scissors	• Watercolors
• A variety of magazines	• Cotton balls
• Colored pencils	• Pens
• Glue	• Crayons

When discussing the exercise with the client, describe it as a way to celebrate and to represent the successful journey the client has traveled along with looking forward to a positive future by creating a movie poster. There is no right or wrong way to construct the poster. It only needs to have meaning for the client. The client need not be in a rush to complete it, and he or she may choose to take it home. In an effort to get the client started or assist in the process, the following questions may be asked.

1. Since we began working together, of what accomplishment are you most proud?

_____

_____

_____

2. What was it about you that helped you reach that goal?

_____

_____

_____

3. What advice would you give to others who are in the same situation you were in when we started therapy?

_____

_____

_____

4. When did you first know that your life was changing for the better?

_____

_____

_____

5. Who were the important people that helped you along the way?

_____

_____

_____

6. How has your sense of yourself changed since we started?

_____

_____

_____

7. What are you looking forward to in the next month? In the next six months?

_____

_____

_____

8. How will you meet the challenges you encounter in the future?

_____

_____

_____

VI.12 Spreading the News: Strengthening New Stories

Therapist's Overview

Purpose of the Exercise

One of the ways of helping change to "stick" is by situating new stories in larger social relationships and contexts. Because clients' problematic stories developed in social contexts, we make arrangements for the social environment to be involved in supporting new stories or identities that emerged in conversations. The purpose of this exercise is to help clients to identify others who might appreciate, encourage, support, and share new stories that engender hope, change, and possibility.

Suggestions for Use

1. This exercise can be used with individuals, couples, families, and groups.
2. This exercise is especially useful when new client stories emerged and as a way of anchoring those new stories in larger contexts.

Exercise

When we experience change for the better, it can be exciting. It means that we are moving forward in our lives and making meaningful gains toward those things that are important to us and improve our lives. Sometimes it can be helpful to share those changes with others, especially those persons who have been or are most supportive of us. This exercise is to help identify those persons and to share the new, exciting news with them. To complete this exercise, please follow the directions below, writing your responses to any questions in the spaces provided.

First, make a list of persons who have been supportive or encouraging of you in the past.

_____   _____

_____   _____

_____   _____

_____   _____

Next, referring back to the list you created, answer the questions below.

1. Who are people who knew you when you were not under the influence of the concern you have been facing who could remind you of your accomplishments and that your life is worth living?

_____   _____

_____   _____

_____   _____

_____   _____

2. Who else needs to know about the stance you have taken to reclaim your life?

_____   _____

_____   _____

_____   _____

_____   _____

3. Who would not be surprised to learn that you gained the upper hand with the concern you have been facing?

_____   _____

_____   _____

_____   _____

_____   _____

4. Who needs to know that you made a commitment to maintaining these changes?

_____   _____

_____   _____

_____   _____

_____   _____

5. What did you learn by doing this exercise?

_____

_____

_____

_____

_____

Consider sharing the changes you made with the persons you listed.

VI.13   *Where Do We Go From Here? Using Original Goals as Benchmarks for Charting a Future Course*

Therapist's Overview

Purpose of the Exercise

Therapeutic progress is defined primarily by the client's subjective experience and evaluation of the effectiveness of services. In the ongoing process of evaluation, the original goals can be used as comparison points for, primarily, the client and, secondarily, the therapist, to collaboratively gauge current progress and to map future plans. While recognizing that initial goals are prone to evolution, they are important in preventing therapy from aimlessly floating adrift. The purpose of this exercise is to facilitate a discussion between the client and therapist that assesses the status of therapy at a particular point in time. If the goals have indeed changed, they should be reestablished according to the same process as was articulated with intake goals. A description of the difference between goals and outcomes should also be included before the exercise so that the broader impact of therapy can be examined.

Suggestions for Use

1. This exercise is intended for clients whose progress appears to have stalled or for those who seem to be preparing for an alteration in services.
2. The exercise can be completed in written form, verbally, or a combination, depending on the needs of the client.
3. It is important to articulate to the client that the introduction of this exercise in no way suggests a clinical articulation that clients are not progressing or that services should be terminated. It is merely a structure for further conversation.
4. Cross-reference: The effectiveness of this exercise will be enhanced if used along with Exercise II.8, "G-O! Focusing on Goals and Outcomes" and Exercise II.14, "From Here to Where? Service Planning for Change."

Exercise

During every therapeutic process, it is important to be constantly evaluating if the service continues to be useful to the client. While initial goals were established, frequently circumstances necessitate a redefinition of them so that both therapist and client are clear on the intent, focus, and benchmarks of successful therapy. Below is a worksheet designed to assist in the evaluation process and to promote this discussion.

Please answer the following questions:

1. What was one of your initial goals for therapy?

_____

_____

2. On a scale of 1 to 10, with 10 being the highest, to what degree have you met this goal?

_____

3. How has therapy affected this score?

_____

_____

4. How has your life been affected as a result of this score?

_____

_____

5. What could be done to raise this score?

_____

_____

6. Is this original score still relevant to your current circumstances? If not, how would you like it to be modified?

_____

_____

Repeat the above questions according to the number of original goals. If new goals are deemed necessary, please see the exercises cited above.

SECTION VII

CREATING A CULTURE OF CARE AND RESPECT
Consultation, Supervision, and Development

VII.1 The Reflective Consultation: A Conversational Approach to Generating Change

Therapist's Overview

Purpose of the Exercise

Clients, therapists, supervisors, and others involved in therapy can become stuck. No matter the intent, there are times when conversations will bog down, become unproductive, or simply come to a standstill. In such cases, it can be helpful to use strategies that introduce new ideas and ways of viewing people and situations. One way of doing this is by using what is often referred to as "reflective" consultation. This process can be used in different contexts with different arrangements of persons to assist with the generation of new ideas. The purpose of this exercise is to learn how to engage in conversations for change to assist with stuck systems.

Suggestions for Use

1. This exercise can be used in therapy with individuals, couples, or families and in supervision, training, or meetings.
2. This exercise can be used for people in or outside of formal therapy. Once the process is learned, it can be useful for generating new ideas in many contexts.
3. This exercise provides an excellent means for training new therapists on how to use strengths-based language.
4. A minimum of three but no more than five people are required for this exercise.

Exercise

This exercise can help to generate new ideas in situations that have become closed-down. Because stuck systems can benefit from an infusion of ideas, reflecting consultations provide a pathway for creating new ideas and directions. The purpose of this exercise is to use conversation as a vehicle for change through a structured process. To complete this exercise, please follow the instructions below.

1. Choose one person to present a stuck situation involving a client or personal situation. The other two or more members will form the team.

2. The person presenting the stuck situation is to take 6 to 10 minutes to focus on the following aspects of the situation:

   a. A brief description of the problem.
   b. What would he or she like to be different or have change about the concern, problem, or difficulty?
   c. What has been tried so far to achieve that change?
   d. What kind of feedback would he or she like from the team?

The presenter may also add other details as time permits. Please try not to exceed the allotted time.

3. During the presentation of the stuck situation, the team is to observe, listen, and take notes. The team is not to ask any questions.

4. When the presenter finishes, the team is to take 4 to 8 minutes to have a conversation among its members. The team is to consider the content areas described in Number 2, adding in what stood out and resonated with each team member. As general guidelines, team members' responses should:

   a. Be from a "not-knowing" position (assuming no prior knowledge about the situation discussed).
   b. Address only what was stated during the presentation.
   c. Highlight strengths.
   d. Be framed from a position of conjecture (i.e., "I was curious," "I wonder," etc.).
   e. Be tentative.

The presenter is not to ask or be asked questions during this process.

5. The presenter then takes 2 to 5 minutes to reflect and convey what resonated with him or her. There is no dialogue between the presenter and team during this process.

6. When the process is complete, the presenter and team take time to debrief and ask whatever questions they have of each other.

7. After completing the exercise, write down any key ideas that came across for you as the presenter or as a team member.

_____

_____

_____

_____

8. Describe what the experience was like for you.

_____

_____

_____

_____

_____

9. What was most and least useful about it?

_____

_____

_____

_____

_____

10. How might this type of consultation be useful to you in the future?

_____

_____

_____

_____

_____

In addition to therapy, it can be helpful to use reflective conversation practices in contexts such as meetings, groups, and trainings.

VII.2   *You Say You Want a Revolution: Taking the Initiative to Cultivate Change*

Therapist's Overview

Purpose of the Exercise

Therapists, particularly those who work in settings and climates in which external factors (e.g., parameters for service provision, limited resources, supervisory relationships, etc.) present challenges, must continuously search for ways of staying focused and effective. It is important to acknowledge hurdles and not let them interfere with or diminish the tasks at hand. While working toward larger institutional and societal changes, one has to keep an eye on what can be done on an individual basis to better the lives of others. The purpose of this exercise is to explore ways that therapists can work to cultivate change at multiple levels while focusing on the most important part of services—clients.

Suggestions for Use

1. This exercise can be used individually by therapists (or those providing mental health or social services) or in group settings. It can also be used in supervision and training.
2. It can be helpful to revisit this exercise periodically.
3. Exercise I.6, "Me, Myself, and I: Understanding Personal Strengths," should be completed prior to this one.
4. Cross-references: See Exercise I.1, "The Philosophical Inventory: Expanding Awareness and Impact of Beliefs" and Exercise I.7, "How I Describe What I Do: Examining Personal Theory and Principles of Change."

Exercise

Every therapist will at some point face challenges that will pose threats to service provision. Although these challenges can vary, one must learn how to work at multiple levels to stimulate change at organizational and social levels. In the midst of this, it is most important not to lose focus on providing the highest quality services to clients. This exercise will help to reorient you toward change at multiple levels through key questions. To complete this exercise, please write your responses to the questions in the spaces provided.

1. Take a few minutes to think about your job. First, consider the benefits—the things you really like about what you do, your setting, and so forth. Make a list of these things under the "+" sign. When you are finished, make a list of the things you experience as challenges or drawbacks of your job under the "–" sign.

+	*Rating*	–	*Rating*
_____	_____	_____	_____
_____	_____	_____	_____
_____	_____	_____	_____

_____ _____   _____ _____

_____ _____   _____ _____

_____ _____   _____ _____

2. Returning to your list, using a scale of 1 to 10, in which 1 represents a major threat and 10 represents a major asset, rate each benefit and drawback.

3. Make a list of the two things in each category with the highest and lowest scores.

Highest

_____ _____   _____ _____

_____ _____   _____ _____

Lowest

_____ _____   _____ _____

_____ _____   _____ _____

4. How might you use the strong points (areas with highest scores) to help deal with the challenges (areas with lowest scores)?

_____

_____

_____

_____

5. Now, take a moment to think about what you do on a regular basis to positively affect changes within your setting. This can be related to coworker relationships, policy, or any aspects of your setting other than direct service provision (although these things are likely to either directly or indirectly affect services). Discuss this below.

_____

_____

_____

_____

6. What do you do on a regular basis to maintain a focus on helping your clients to the best of your ability despite the challenges you face?

_____

_____

_____

_____

_____

7. What do you do when you are feeling worn down or depleted?

_____

_____

_____

_____

_____

8. Referring to your responses in Exercise I.6, "Me, Myself, and I: Understanding Personal Strengths," what personal strengths can you tap into to help meet the challenges described in Question 7?

_____

_____

_____

_____

_____

Remember that actually maintaining a commitment to change can be the most significant challenge a therapist can face. It is an everyday, ongoing process that involves perseverance in the face of things that may take time to change. Consider how you can use your internal and external resources to stay the course.

VII.3 Bringing Out the Best: Assessing Organizational Strengths

Therapist's Overview

Purpose of the Exercise

Organizations that provide effective services utilize processes to identify their strengths and areas of growth. They also develop plans for employing their strengths to meet those challenges. The purpose of this exercise is to explore how organizations can assess their capacities to meet both internal and external challenges.

Suggestions for Use

1. This exercise can be used in small or large meetings, trainings, and on an individual basis.
2. It can be helpful to revisit this exercise periodically.
3. Cross-references: See Exercise I.1, "The Philosophical Inventory: Expanding Awareness and Impact of Beliefs," Exercise I.6, "Me, Myself, and I: Understanding Personal Strengths," and Exercise I.7, "How I Describe What I Do: Examining Personal Theory and Principles of Change."

Exercise

Just as individuals have strengths and areas of growth, so do organizations. One of the ways organizations can meet both internal and external challenges is by employing processes to assess these areas. This exercise is to help organizations explore their capacities and determine areas in need of growth and development to enhance their services. This exercise can be used on an individual or group (i.e., meetings, staffings, and so on) basis. To complete this exercise, please write your individual responses to the questions or those developed by your group in the spaces provided.

1. Make a list of the strengths of your organization. For each strength, rate the area on a scale of 1 to 10 (with 1 being the weakest and 10 the strongest). Then, think of an area within that strength upon which you could improve. Name the "Area of Growth," and finally grade yourself in that area according to how you feel improvements are progressing.

For example:

Strength	(score)	Area of Growth	(score)
Communication	7	Staff Development	5

(1)

Strength	(score)	Area of Growth	(score)

(2)

Strength	(score)	Area of Growth	(score)

(3)

Strength	**(score)**	**Area of Growth**	**(score)**
_____	_____	_____	_____

(4)

Strength	**(score)**	**Area of Growth**	**(score)**
_____	_____	_____	_____

(5)

Strength	**(score)**	**Area of Growth**	**(score)**
_____	_____	_____	_____

(6)

Strength	**(score)**	**Area of Growth**	**(score)**
_____	_____	_____	_____

2. Make a list of the weaknesses and areas growth within your organization. After you complete this, using a scale of 1 to 10, in which 1 represents a minimal weakness and 10 represents a major weakness, rate each.

–	*Rating*
_____	_____
_____	_____
_____	_____
_____	_____
_____	_____
_____	_____
_____	_____
_____	_____
_____	_____

3. List the top three scores in each grouping.

—	*Rating*
_____	_____
_____	_____
_____	_____
_____	_____
_____	_____
_____	_____
_____	_____
_____	_____
_____	_____

4. Either individually or as a group, consider how the strengths of your organization can be used to meet the weaknesses and areas of growth. Write your findings below.

_____

_____

_____

_____

_____

_____

_____

_____

_____

5. Beyond the already existing strengths of your organization, what is needed to better meet the challenges listed?

_____

_____

_____

_____

_____

Going a step further, discuss the following questions with members of your organization.

1. What gives us spirit and life?

_____

_____

_____

_____

_____

2. Who contributes to that spirit and life?

_____

_____

_____

_____

_____

3. What are five small things we can do as an organization to better develop our sense of spirit in the coming weeks and months?

a. _____

b. _____

c. _____

d. _____

e. _____

4. How will we ensure that this happens?

_____

_____

_____

_____

_____

Make plans to revisit what was discussed during this exercise. Be sure to address progress and hurdles to putting what was discussed into action. In addition, consider the following points:

- Every organization has strengths and something that works.
- What is focused on and given attention to becomes a socially constructed reality.
- There are many perspectives and ways of understanding the same situation.
- Inquiry, the act of asking questions of an organization or group, influences groups in some way.
- Respect toward others and in relationships facilitates cooperation.
- The past informs but does not determine the future—bring forward the best from the past.
- Envision the future.

VII.4   *Putting Out the Fire: How Supervisors Can Help Stave Off Burnout*

Therapist's Overview

Purpose of the Exercise

Providing therapeutic services can be thrilling, inspiring, and engaging. It can also be exhausting, stressful, and draining. For a supervisor, the signs of burnout in a supervisee can be as clear as a frown on his or her face. As a matter of personal fulfillment and professional effectiveness, it is crucial that a supervisor not only recognize the signs of burnout, but also possess the tools capable of helping his or her supervisees through such difficult times. Many styles of supervision bear a strong resemblance to those used when working with clients. However, differing considerations are necessary during professional supervision. The following exercise is meant as a guide to help the burning out employee reconnect with his or her core philosophy and rediscover the passion and meaning in work.

Suggestions for Use

1. As with clients, it is important to allow the supervisee to be the primary director of the conversation. In these situations, the line between the personal and professional can become blurry. Should this arise, continually emphasize the interplay between the two.
2. This exercise can be used at any point during supervision with therapists of any experience level.
3. Cross-reference: This exercise may be enhanced through use in collaboration with Exercise I.5, "Composing Your Theoretical Worldview: What I Believe."

Exercise

Everyone experiences stress. In fact, a certain degree of stress can be a productive motivator. However, too much stress can lead to declining physical health, lack of motivation, and general unhappiness. During such times, it can be helpful to remind ourselves of that which at one time provided nourishment for our professional lives. Below are a series of questions intended to help you begin to light your inner fire anew.

1. Please list the aspects of your job that excited you the most when you first started.

_____

_____

_____

_____

_____

2. How does this list reflect the personal philosophy you brought with you to this job?

_____

_____

_____

_____

_____

3. On a scale of 1 to 10, with 10 being the best, how fulfilled or satisfied are you currently in your job?

_____

4. What do you remember as being your first fulfilling experience in this job?

_____

_____

_____

_____

_____

5. On a scale of 1 to 10, with 10 being the best, how did this experience make you feel?

_____

6. How did this experience reflect your personal philosophy?

_____

_____

_____

_____

_____

7. If you were to have a similar experience to that described above, on a scale of 1 to 10, how fulfilled or satisfied would you feel?

_____

8. What strategies can you and I use to bring your overall score closer to where it once was, or perhaps higher?

_____

_____

_____

_____

_____

9. How will you know when your job has regained its satisfaction for you?

_____

_____

_____

_____

_____

VII.5   *Effectively Using an Airplane Oxygen Mask: Practicing Self-Care First*

Therapist's Overview

Purpose of the Exercise

If you have ever been on a plane, you can probably recall what flight attendants say when illustrating how to use the oxygen masks. It is something like "put the oxygen mask first on yourself before helping someone else." At first this statement might seem a little selfish, especially for helping professionals who make it a career to help others. However, it does make perfect sense; before you can help someone else you need to be in a healthy position yourself. The purpose of this exercise is to examine your self-care techniques and ensure you are in the best possible position to help others, regardless of your role.

Suggestions for Use

1. The exercise could benefit counselors, supervisors, and office managers. It also could be used during staff trainings and orientations.
2. It also could be modified and used with clients and families to assess their self-care.

Exercise

Perhaps another way to frame this exercise is with the phrase "preventative medicine is the best medicine." This exercise will provide the individual with the needed preventative medicine to remain effective while working and also means to reduce the chances of burnout in times of stress and heavy workloads. The following are some suggestions to think about to remain as effective as possible.

1. If you have not done so already, examine the many roles in your life and what is needed to be effective in those roles. We all fulfill many roles throughout our lives—roles that require true diligence. If you know your roles and the energy needed in each role, you may have a better chance of prioritizing your day and better utilizing your energy.

   What did you learn by examining the roles in your life?

   _____

   _____

2. Knowing your roles is one thing and establishing boundaries between roles is the next step in remaining healthy. One way I establish boundaries is to keep work at work and embrace my home life when not working. This might not work for everyone, and others may find it extremely beneficial to work from home. The point here is to find what works best for you and to become in tune with your needs.

How might you do this a little more in the future?

_____

_____

_____

_____

_____

3. Knowing your body is another beneficial task to ensuring healthy functioning. Discover when you do your best work (morning, after lunch, late night) and capitalize on your own effectiveness.

When do you typically do your best work?

_____

_____

_____

_____

_____

4. Perhaps the greatest preventive remedy is knowing when to say "no." If we know our roles, boundaries, and how we operate most efficiently, then it may become easier to know our limits and say no to things that may make us become less effective. If we are unable to say no, it is like putting the oxygen mask on others first and neglecting your needs.

How can you set a few more limits for yourself such that you are able to be as engaged and effective as you would like to be?

_____

_____

_____

_____

_____

How might this benefit you?

_____

_____

_____

_____

_____

How could you get this to happen a little more in the future?

_____

_____

_____

_____

_____

VII.6 The Windmill: Generating Energy Through Congruence

Therapist's Overview

Purpose of the Exercise

The concept of "balance" runs through many philosophies, religions, and theories. A universal theme associated with balance is the notion of connection to self, others (relationships), nature (biological world), and spirituality (or higher power). It can be said that the more connectedness there is, the higher degree of balance the person experiences. As therapists, these forms of connection can be beneficial in countering burnout, increasing job satisfaction, and contributing to career longevity. Furthermore, a higher degree of connectedness can have a windmill-like effect, generating more energy, which is essential to facing the challenges of life and work. The purpose of this exercise is to explore how therapists can achieve higher levels of connectedness.

Suggestions for Use

1. This exercise can be used as a stand-alone exercise in supervision, meetings, and groups.
2. It can be helpful to revisit this exercise periodically.
3. Cross-references: see Exercise I.1, "The Philosophical Inventory: Expanding Awareness and Impact of Beliefs"; Exercise I.6, "Me, Myself, and I: Understanding Personal Strengths"; and Exercise I.7, "How I Describe What I Do: Examining Personal Theory and Principles of Change."

Exercise

We sometimes need to expel disproportionate amounts of energy to address what is in need of immediate attention. The concern is that we do not always move back to "center" and toward balance. It can therefore be helpful to take a step back and revisit our connectedness to ourselves, others, and other meaningful things such as nature and spirituality. This exercise is to help you to reorient to areas that can help to reenergize and revitalize you. This, in effect, can create a "windmill" of sorts in which you actually gain energy by employing small but essential strategies. To complete this exercise, please write your individual responses to the questions or those developed by your group in the spaces provided.

1. What do you consider to be the most important areas of connection in your life (to what and to whom)?

_____

_____

_____

_____

_____

2. What are the areas in which you feel at times you expel too much energy and perhaps are more energy draining than energy giving?

_____

_____

_____

_____

_____

3. List three things that help to bring you back to "center" and a better degree of balance.

    a. _____

    b. _____

    c. _____

4. Reflect on the following points and consider how you can build on them to create more momentum and energy in your life and work.

- Believe in what you do and "walk the talk" (do what you say).
- Take action and make good on your word.
- Be a source of energy for others.
- Be a source of optimism and support to others; hope is contagious.
- Give your unconditional energies (body, mind, heart, and soul).
- Be strengths based, not just "positive."
- Recognize others' contributions to change.
- Be a resource to others (i.e., clients, staff, etc.).
- Check in with yourself regularly. (Ask yourself: What kind of day did I have? What else is going on with me?)
- Build in restorative recovery time every day.
- Find what inspires you and gives you hope.

5. What is one small thing you can do to achieve more energy and balance in your life?

_____

_____

_____

_____

_____

6. What is the first thing you can do to make this happen a little bit after you complete this exercise?

_____

_____

_____

_____

_____

Over the next few weeks, notice your levels of energy and the things that seem to affect it positively and negatively. Revisit the points in Question #4 as needed to reconnect with yourself, others, and the world.

VII.7 The Inner Mister Rogers: Cultivating Acceptance and Compassion During Supervision

Therapist's Overview

Purpose of the Exercise

Since Carl Rogers spoke of "unconditional positive regard," it has become a fundamental premise underlying many therapeutic approaches. While the concept has been further developed and adapted as later models and approaches arose, Roger's description of the necessity of genuine respect and empathy for the client is today nearly universally accepted. This, however, is not always easy. No matter the experience or skill level, most therapists will at some point in their careers encounter a client whom, despite their best efforts, they perhaps secretly label as resistant, manipulative, or worse. As supervisors, it is important to warn of these pitfalls and to assist the therapist in rediscovering their client's basic human dignity. As discussed elsewhere, this point of view is essential for the clinician to be as effective as possible in the therapeutic relationship.

Suggestions for Use

1. This exercise can be used at any time during supervision in both professional and academic settings.
2. It may be adapted for use with clients who feel "stuck" in a relationship to a particular individual.
3. Cross-references: This exercise may also be used together with Exercise I.1, "The Philosophical Inventory: Expanding Awareness and Impact of Beliefs" and "Walking the Talk: Employing a Strengths and Solution-Focused Philosophy."

Exercise

If dreams tell us anything, it is that most things can be interpreted in multiple ways. This is particularly true of human behavior. As complicated creatures ("I contain multitudes," said Walt Whitman), our actions can at one moment be seen as altruistic and the next seen as the height of selfishness. When working with our clients, we can sometimes get comfortable with one type of interpretation for multiple actions. This can blind us to other possibilities and lead to a sense of "stuckness" for both you and your client. The following are some questions for us to discuss together during our supervision.

1. Name of the client with whom you are frustrated.

_____

2. Identify the main action your client has taken recently with which you are struggling.

_____

_____

_____

3. Name three different possible motivations or interpretations of this action.

a. _____

_____

b. _____

_____

c. _____

_____

4. Which of those interpretations do you feel is the most likely to be true?

_____

_____

_____

5. Which of those interpretations do you consider to be the most compassionate toward your client?

_____

_____

_____

6. Which of those options offers the most options and possibilities for change?

_____

_____

_____

7. How do you feel you can be most helpful to this client in the future?

_____

_____

_____

VII.8   The Benefits of Self-Reflection: Maximizing Counselor Effectiveness

Therapist's Overview

Purpose of the Exercise

The intent of this exercise is for the counselor to remain self-reflective and beneficent to the client. It is imperative for the counselor to have a continuous collaborative orientation to reflect, assess, and plan the counseling process. Simple self questions can be asked by the counselor to remain vigilant to this task. When a counselor sees a client slipping into old patterns of behavior or not responding to a specific technique or exercise, one could ask "How am I responding to this person in ways that are not completely beneficial?" Perhaps you are asking the client to do things he or she is not ready to do. A goal of reflective practice is to continuously question your practice and find means to rigorously answer your question with the end result of improved practice.

Suggestions for Use

1. This exercise can be beneficial both as a tool for beginning counselors to develop self-reflective skills and as a tool to be utilized during supervision.
2. This exercise could be useful when you feel yourself possibly maintaining the status quo or when you notice diminished client progress.

Exercise

A successful beginning to this exercise would start when reviewing case notes and planning for future sessions. The following are some simple questions you can ask yourself to increase your self-reflective skills.

1. If I believe a client is being resistant, what role did I play in that process?

_____

_____

2. What do I need to accomplish not to respond to my client in the same ways that ineffective counselors have?

_____

_____

3. How can I maintain or increase collaboration with my client?

_____

_____

4. What parts of your counseling illustrate it is an effective session?

_____

_____

5. What happens during your counseling that may indicate you are not as effective as you would like?

_____

_____

6. What would the client say to illustrate that he or she no longer needs counseling?

_____

_____

7. What do I need to do to make that happen?

_____

_____

8. How can I use supervision to reflect, assess, and plan the remainder of the sessions?

_____

_____

VII.9   Interviewing Your Supervisor: Is Your Supervisor as Strengths and Solution-Focused as You Are?

Therapist's Overview

Purpose of the Exercise

The key to the work of the supervisor and supervisee is one of the hallmarks of strengths and solution-based (SSB) therapy—a focus on relationship. It is vital, therefore, for the supervisee to develop a clear, up-front understanding of the personal philosophy and working style of their supervisor. The more overt conversations regarding such matters take place as quickly into the working relationship as possible, the more quickly and deeply the two working parties can grow together. The purpose of this is to give the new supervisee a series of important questions to be asked of their new superior. The process will facilitate a collaborative relation and suggest a dialogue structure that empowers both parties to actively articulate their questions and needs.

Suggestions for Use

1. This exercise is intended for use toward the beginning of the supervision relationship.
2. The interviewer is encouraged to share his or her own opinions to the questions and pursue follow-up questions as they become relevant.
3. Cross-reference: This activity can be used in conjunction with Exercise I.1, "The Philosophical Inventory: Expanding Awareness and Impact of Beliefs."

Exercise

As we begin working together, it is vital that I understand your point of view and philosophy as well as you do mine. Hopefully this is the beginning of an ongoing discussion that will result in continued growth and development for us both. Please answer the following questions:

1. What does the term "strengths and solution-focused" mean to you?

_____

_____

_____

2. How would you describe your philosophy as a supervisor?

_____

_____

_____

3. What will you use to evaluate my development as a clinician?

_____

_____

_____

4. What or who has had the greatest impact on your learning?

_____

_____

_____

5. What have been your greatest challenges in incorporating strengths and solution-focused ideas into your work?

_____

_____

_____

6. What are your strengths as a supervisor?

_____

_____

_____

7. What are your areas of growth as a supervisor?

_____

_____

8. Please give an example of a client who achieved great success using the strengths and solution-focused philosophy.

_____

_____

_____

9. What is something you would like me to know that will help me understand your manner of working?

_____

_____

_____

10. Is there a question I should have asked that I did not?

_____

_____

_____

VII.10   Reinventing the Cookbook: Proactive and Reflective Ways to Use This Book

Therapist's Overview

Purpose of the Exercise

Perhaps the most essential skill for a counselor to develop is his or her ability to become a reflective practitioner. A reflective practitioner actively reflects and critiques his or her practice. Moreover, the reflective practitioner has the skills to implement change and assess its effectiveness. Thus, a reflective practitioner engages in a continual process of self-investigation with the end result of improved practice and better service provision.

The intent of this exercise is to help facilitate reflective practitioner skills and create an effective plan to utilize this book. The purpose of this book is not to be a quick fix or to be used as a cookbook with predetermined exercises to meet every counseling situation. Rather, this book is to be used as a tool to examine your and your client's strengths to determine the most effective course of action.

Suggestions for Use

1. This exercise is most appropriate as a tool to plan and reflect on sessions.
2. This exercise can also be utilized in supervision or as a teaching model for new counselors.
3. When you are in doubt about how a session is going, ask your client. This is a simple way to become process and outcome informed.
4. Cross-reference: This exercise can also be utilized with the last section in the Introduction, "We Are Only as Strong as Our Weakest Link: Strengthening the Use of This Book."

Exercise

To begin this exercise, page through this book and get a "feel" for its content and think about how it resonates with your ideas of change. Ask yourself what makes sense and what needs further clarification. Jot down your thoughts and questions and begin a dialogue with your supervisor or another colleague. Use your conversations as a basis to critically reflect on the how and why of your counseling (i.e., How do I counsel and why do I engage clients this way?). If you feel you need more work in this area, complete exercise I.5, "Composing Your Theoretical Worldview: What I Believe."

To continue this exercise, think about a particular client and ask yourself the following questions:

1. What is going well with Client X?

_____

_____

2. How do you know it is going well?

_____

_____

3. What is needed to make your next session just a little bit better?

_____

_____

4. What aspect of this book could be used to maximize the above questions?

_____

_____

5. What could be improved with Client X?

_____

_____

6. How do you know it could be improved?

_____

_____

7. What is needed in your next session to improve it just a little bit?

_____

_____

8. What aspect of this book could be used to maximize your answers in Questions 5 through 7?

_____

_____

Index